Your Towns and Ci.

Hull

in the Great War
1914–1919

Your Towns and Cities in the Great War

Hull
in the Great War
1914–1919

David Bilton

Pen & Sword
MILITARY

Dedicated to the memory of
Louis Tertocha
23 September 1954 – 11 October 2013

* * *

First published in Great Britain in 2015 by
PEN & SWORD MILITARY
an imprint of
Pen and Sword Books Ltd
47 Church Street, Barnsley
South Yorkshire S70 2AS

ISBN 978 1 47382 314 3

A CIP record for this book is available from the British Library

Printed and bound in England
by CPI Group (UK) Ltd, Croydon, CR0 4YY

Typeset in Times New Roman by Chic Graphics

Pen & Sword Books Ltd incorporates the imprints of
Pen & Sword Archaeology, Atlas, Aviation, Battleground, Discovery,
Family History, History, Maritime, Military, Naval, Politics, Railways,
Select, Social History, Transport, True Crime, Claymore Press,
Frontline Books, Leo Cooper, Praetorian Press, Remember When,
Seaforth Publishing and Wharncliffe.

For a complete list of Pen and Sword titles please contact
Pen and Sword Books Limited
47 Church Street, Barnsley, South Yorkshire, S70 2AS, England
E-mail: enquiries@pen-and-sword.co.uk
Website: www.pen-and-sword.co.uk

Contents

Acknowledgements

A really big thank you to the staff of the Hull History Centre for their untiring kindness, help and assistance in the research for this book. As usual Anne Coulson kindly read and checked the manuscript. While, as an ex-Hull resident from birth, many of the illustrations come from my own family, I owe a number of people thanks for their contribution: Alex Duke, a Cottingham historian; Malcolm Mann, avid local historian who provided a considerable number of rare illustrations; Kenneth Durkin, who provided both information and photos; Sheila Boynton; and the late Kathleen Osler. Thank you.

The home of William Wilberforce, the slavery abolitionist.

47251 HULL. WILBERFORCE HOUSE.

Introduction

The war memorial for those local men who died in the South African War at the turn of the century.

Following boundary changes and natural growth, the population of Hull was 123,408 in 1901; ten years later at the last census before the war, it stood at 275,486. This growth was made possible by new industries, railways and the rapid growth of the shipping industry brought about by increased world trade. The older industries included linseed oil and paint manufacture. A long-established and major business was brewing, dominated at the turn of the century by just two companies, Hull Brewery and Moors' and Robson's. In terms of numbers employed, the important new industries were the glue and starch works of the Reckitt family. The initial products were rapidly diversified to make the company international.

Trawler fishing had developed throughout most of the century, helping to make Hull an important fishing port and enhance its maritime status. Even though steam trawlers needed fewer crew it still employed nearly 1,500 men and would provide many of the crew and the boats for minesweeping for the Royal Navy during the war: trawlers were ideal boats for the job, the crews knew the areas they would work in and the war meant they could not fish anyway. In total, the Humber area provided 880 vessels and around 9,000 men.

Following the fishing industry's growth, ancillary industries grew up which, in fact, employed more men than did the trawlers. These included fish curing and processing, ice manufacture, cod liver oil manufacture and fish manure production.

A postcard showing the coat of arms of the city of Kingston-upon-Hull. Its significance is unclear but it has been in use since the early 1400s.

King Edward Street around the turn of the century. In the background can be seen the Dock Offices and the William Wilberforce statue.

The Hull trawler fleet was used to danger at sea. In 1909 they had been shelled by the Russian Fleet in the North Sea that believed them to be Japanese naval ships. This shows the damage to the stern of the trawler Moulmein.

Victoria pier on a busy day. This was the start of the crossing to the Lincolnshire shore.

By the end of the nineteenth century, corn milling had grown from small independent millers to large companies, such as Rank, using steam mills and roller-grinding. This growth fuelled the import of foreign grain which benefited from relatively low dock dues and competitive railway rates, and made Hull a centre for grain arriving for other parts of the country. By 1911, imports were nearly 900,000 tons a year.

Running from Hull to Selby, where it joined the line to Leeds, the railway connected Hull with the West Riding. By 1849, Hull was only ten hours from London. Its success brought further development and the original station was replaced by the present Paragon station. The arrival of the ferry to New Holland cut travel time to London down to seven hours. With the planned development of east coast resorts, rail travel increased dramatically and the railways grew.

Side by side with the development of the railways came the increase in dock space. Junction Dock from 1829 was followed in 1846 by Railway Dock and Victoria Dock in 1850. Between 1869 and 1883 three further docks were built: the Albert Dock in 1869; the William Wright dock in 1880; and St Andrew's in 1883, which became the fishing dock and moved the industry to Hessle Road. The resulting price war between the companies involved benefited the ship-owners and the town's merchants. Before the war started, two further docks were constructed: Riverside in 1907 and King George in 1914. Although goods in Hull arrived from around the world, most of its trade came from the Baltic and northern Europe. At the start of the war, the port of Hull was third after London and Liverpool; its tonnage was 4,705,000 in 1913.

Two other products helped Hull's economy: emigrants and coal. The Wilson line transported thousands of Scandinavians, Russians and Eastern Europeans who were looking for a better life, or in the case of Jewish migrants, escaping from persecution. These migrants landed in Hull and were very quickly transported on to Liverpool on their way to North America. Coal seams near Doncaster and Thorne were exploited between 1900 and 1910. Their closeness to Hull made it the economic choice for sending coal abroad as well as directly by rail to Hull. The size of the trade is shown by the tonnage shipped in 1913, over 4.5 million tons.

The port's prosperity was at a zenith as the war began. 1913 had been a record for shipping tonnage at 6,692,000 and wheat imports reached almost a million tons in 1912. Hull's economy was affected immediately the war began. Boats were held in German ports and some were unable to reach their destination. All trade with Germany, a major exporter through Hull, ceased, and trade with Russia was greatly reduced. By 1918, wheat imports were less than 250,000 tons, coal and

Quayside in Hull. By the start of the war it was the third biggest, by tonnage, of the UK ports.

The relatively new City Hall, advertising a tramway men's band concert. On the right is the Prudential Building destroyed in The Blitz.

Victoria Square in the city centre showing the dock offices and Queen Victoria's statue.

VICTORIA SQUARE. HULL.

other exports also fell as did the shipping tonnage. With the requisitioning of trawlers for mine-sweeping and submarine detection work, the fishing fleet suffered. Less than a quarter were left for fishing and regardless of their role during the war, losses in ships and men were high. Many Hull-owned ships were sunk, resulting in the merging of the Wilson and Ellerman lines.

Hand-in-hand with business development went some urban improvement, notably the provision of clean water from Anlaby that saved many lives, and a public park, Pearson Park, given by Alderman Pearson in 1860. This was followed by a public cemetery and road widening in the Old Town. Then came improvements in sanitation, although not without considerable effort by campaigners like William Hunt, editor of the *Eastern Morning News*. Its description of life on Hessle Road in an advanced nation like Britain is difficult to believe. The area was compared with the foulest slums in Constantinople, where space was shared with livestock, 'sewage flowed from decrepit privies' and there was 'widespread abuse of women and children, of prostitution and incest.'

During the 1870s the infantile diarrhoea rate averaged 237 per thousand. Thirty years later it was 311 and rising. The rate payers

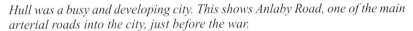
Hull was a busy and developing city. This shows Anlaby Road, one of the main arterial roads into the city, just before the war.

refused to pay for the conversion to water closets of the privies that were causing the disease. At the start of the war, therefore, the housing of the working-classes of Hull was little improved on eighty years previously.

Education was also an issue. There were only three School Board 'higher-grade' schools before the end of the nineteenth century, well-equipped but short of qualified staff; only the middle-classes received secondary education. In the public sector, even after the 1902 Education Act class sizes were enormous and the schools badly underfunded. Hull also lagged behind in technical, commercial and teacher training education.

As part of the 1897 Jubilee celebrations, Hull was granted city status. It had a built-up area radiating out along the main roads for up to three miles. There were working-class suburbs and newer areas of middle-class housing, the richer merchants having left the city for the villages west of Hull. Transport around the city was made easier, first by horse-drawn, then steam-powered, and finally electric trams. Numerous grand public buildings were erected in the first years of the twentieth century and by 1900 most of the Queen's Dock area squalor had gone. In the east, Sir James Reckitt initiated the development of the Garden Village, 'setting much higher housing standards for future developments to follow'. In the west, new developments continued into the early war years.

Spring Bank in Edwardian times showing a wide street split by a row of trees with a tram in the distance.

In June 1914 the King and Queen visited the new Hull dock named after him.

Granted a licence to operate a telephone system in 1902, Hull was and still is the only independent telephone operator in the country. This independence provided the city with much needed money during the war. 'Hull lacked the really wealthy families of places like Liverpool, Manchester and the West Riding and most members of the local council were from the middle and lower ranks of business and tradesmen. The workforce was characterised by dock related work. Over 35 per cent had jobs such as unloading ships, quayside activities, warehousing and shipyard engineering and a significant group of unskilled casual workers, typical of any port but…often out of work in winter because of Hull's trade with the frozen Baltic ports. Hull was a poor town compared with other similar places in the British Isles and many wealthy families had moved to the East Riding to live in style.'

How did the above factors contribute to the large number of recruits raised in Hull? In simple terms, the war disrupted life in a profound way. 'It disrupted the major industries like fishing as well as others depending on the Baltic Trade from which it took decades to recover. In addition, for the duration of the war, the government diverted cargo from Hull because of the strategic risk of enemy attack. With so many

Holy Trinity Church in the centre of the city is the largest parish church in England. It survived the bombing of the city in two world wars.

dependent on the docks for work, the War had an immediate impact on livelihoods and acted as an incentive for young men to join up.'

Figures show the rapid reduction in work. 'For the business community 1914 was not a bad year, but naturally not as good as 1913 when 6,151,000 tons of shipping had used the port. In 1914 the decline went no further than 5,307,000 tons. With a full year of war, 1915 was worse and the tonnage was down to 4,060,000. The Baltic was virtually closed, and the docks.'

Imports of timber dropped to just over a half and many Wilson Line ships were trapped in Petrograd. This would help explain why Hull's reputation as a recruiting area was so high.

Residents in Hull were able to keep up to date with world and local events through the *Eastern Morning News* and the *Hull Daily Mail* in the evening, as well as the national dailies. There was also a weekly paper, the *Hull Times*, which covered news from across the East Riding and north Lincolnshire, with different editions focussing more on one area. This book is based on contemporary articles from these papers.

In this narrative there are stories of great heroism, patriotism – like that of Max Schultz, a British spy – and duty; at the other end of the spectrum of life, petty squabbles, drunkenness and murder. Life does not follow a linear path. The trivial and the deeply serious exist side-by-side, hand-in-hand. Sometimes the stories in this book are chronological, at other times grouped, related, linked across the year. In some cases they are one-offs, perhaps they stand alone, and sometimes they are visited again in a different context. They may be flippant, serious, statistical, trivial or of no apparent consequence. That they appear after each other is in no way meant to detract from the personal and national struggle they portray.

National papers provided international and national news, and the local papers explained how and what local people felt. Life is a messy business; the local papers gave a warts-and-all view of real life, with no air-brushing. What is gleaned from local papers is a picture of daily life, the experience of many reflecting how they saw the war, how they behaved and what they felt at the highest, lowest,

Charles Charlton from Paull, near Hull, pictured before the war. A young man without a care, one of the many who joined the army and did not return. He was killed in 1916.

A wedding celebration in Anlaby during the summer of 1913. A year later the young man circled, the writer's grandfather, would be one of the first Hull volunteers for Kitchener's New Army. Also in the photo are his brothers. Five went to war and five returned.

East Park.

As part of the city's development, green spaces were created by public benefactors and Hull Corporation. East Park was provided by the council.

saddest and happiest times in their war. I have tried to show that normal life in Hull was often mundane, that the war, while being all-pervasive, often touched people's lives, with the exception of death and disability, only in transient, temporary ways.

In many cases there seemed to be no war going on because nothing had really changed, or was the situation just slightly different? If you were already hungry, how would rationing affect you? If you had no job, no shelter, how were you affected?

What is also interesting is that the same war did not always have the same effect across the country. While it is obvious that Hull and for example, Reading, were in the same war on the surface, underneath the differences are considerable. Why, when both were essentially working class should there be such differences? Perhaps the underlying message is that, no matter when or why, 'there's nowt so queer as folk'.

CHAPTER 1

1914:
Eager for a Fight

What was life like in Hull just before the war? On the same day as the Austro-Hungarian populace were informed of the partial mobilisation of the army, the 25 July 1914 edition of the *Hull Times*, like other weekly newspapers, concentrated more on local events, leaving the dailies to report on world affairs. While most were aware of the

George Street showing the statue of Andrew Marvell, the famous Metaphysical poet and politician. It was placed there in 1902 and moved twenty years later.

Inside St Mary's Church in Lowgate. The church dates back to the fourteenth century.

Keen to emulate their brothers, fathers, uncles and cousins, these boys show determination to be involved.

assassination in Sarajevo, any war in the Balkans, and there had been previous wars in the area, would surely be of no consequence to Hull.

As war preparations were under way in Europe, the *Hull Times* of 25 July contained its usual wide range of articles that give a flavour of what was important locally, and, that very week, Hull's population was stated as being 291,118. It included two military stories, both local and neither concerned the coming war. During a Territorial Drumhead service in the Pleasure Gardens at Skegness, Corporal Barwis, of the motor-cycle section of the Lincolnshire Yeomanry, was taken suddenly ill and expired almost immediately. He was overcome by the great heat. Across Europe it was a hot summer. The second story was also about part-time soldiers, this time the Lincolnshire Regiment Territorials. At the Humber Bank Range at Barton, shooting at distances of 200 and 500 yards, Barton G Company beat Scunthorpe E Company by 134 points. The best shot of the match was Captain Wilson of the Barton Company.

Other local news included railways, wills, housing, traffic, the Yorkshire Show, theft, violence and murder. On the national and international scene there were stories of the Ulster Conference, violence, death and shipping.

What did the paper tell its readers about these stories? Railways were an important means of transport and essential to Hull's economy, so the 1913 statistics for Britain's rail network were provided. It was reported that there were 40,689 (open) miles of track and 14,749 miles of sidings. Over the year, 1,228,315,000 passengers had been carried, consisting of 256,705,000 workmen, 933,408,000 3rd Class, 12,088,000 2nd Class and 20,025,000 1st Class – where the others came from was not explained. There were 595,000 season ticket holders. Rail freight included 371,571,000 tons of coal, general merchandise and other minerals with receipts of £65,617,000. Total receipts were £124,750,000. To achieve these figures locomotives had run 627,779,000 miles. The biggest wills of the week were those of Miss Lizzie Drummond of 19 Washington Street, who left £1,248 7s 6d gross and Mr Frederick Lambert of 143 Anlaby Road whose estate was valued at £1,042 3s 9d.

As in most towns and cities, there was a shortage of housing in Hull. To alleviate this, Hull Corporation Health Committee decided on a scheme costing £107,270 for laying out the George Street area under *The Housing for the Working Classes Act*. The intention was to provide

252 dwellings. Decisions were made to rebuild Stakes Bridge at Preston, extend the water pipe along Ings Road, to allow Mr Reckitt to build cottages at Sutton, and for Misses A. and F. Mason to build houses in Willerby. A discussion took place on a new reservoir in connection with the North Ferriby and Swanland waterworks.

Another issue common to larger towns and cities was the increasing number of vehicles. In response, councils started taking traffic censuses. Sculcoates RDC reported the results of its census taken from 11-17 July on the Hull to Anlaby and the Hull to Aldborough main roads. The total vehicle numbers were 13,596 and 13,455 respectively.

A new record attendance of 120,000 was set at the Yorkshire Show. Over £3,000 in prizes was awarded to competitors such as J. Deighton of Harrogate, who was the best at shoeing horses; Miss Sarah Mudd of Slade House, Darley, who was the Best Butter Maker in the class 'Yorkshire farmer's wife, sons, or daughter who had not attended the Hemsley or Garforth Dairy Schools'; J. Jackson of Doncaster, who exhibited Melbourne Dray King, judged as the best Shire Horse foaled in 1912; and F. Miller of Birkenhead, whose Shorthorn Bull, Gainford

The land for the first public park in Hull was given by Zachariah Pearson in 1862.

Civilian life continued regardless of the war. An advert for The Grand Café and a reference to Hull Fair.

Royal, was the best in the class of Shorthorns above two and not exceeding three years old.

A respectable twenty-year-old solicitor's clerk, Ben Empson, pleaded guilty to stealing thirty-seven boxes of cigars and one box of cigarettes valued at £24 16s 3d. Although the crime was seen as serious by the bench, for unexplained mitigating circumstances the Chairman only placed him on probation.

Alcohol and violence are close bed-fellows. 'A sordid crime was committed in a public house, the Lion Inn, on Francis Street, ...as a result of which a woman named Sarah Coates' was in a serious condition at Hull infirmary. In the dock was Frederick Harrison, a mariner, charged with unlawfully cutting and wounding with intent to do her grievous bodily harm. He admitted to the crime but claimed he was worse for drink and had been drinking with her.

An accountant, John Thompson, on leave from Africa, provided the most sensational story in the paper. Declared medically fit to stand trial but then found unfit at the trial, he was remanded to Hedon gaol for eight days while further tests were completed. He was charged with the wilful murder of his wife, Hilda, aged twenty-nine, and his two sons, Joseph, aged two, and Donald, just eleven months old. He had shot them and then attempted suicide but the bullet had only damaged his optic nerve leaving him blind. As attempting suicide was a crime he was also charged for his failed suicide. He denied all charges.

The trial ran for some time and appeared in every edition of the paper. In November, at York Assizes, he was found to be insane and detained at His Majesty's pleasure. What had brought him to commit this crime? He had been falsely charged in Africa but acquitted. However, he had been ruined by this and had no job. With no money or job prospects, he took a rational and logical decision and murdered his family. He was found guilty of all charges, declared insane and not responsible for his actions and placed in custody as a criminal lunatic.

However, a week later, after the Austro-Hungarian declaration of war on Serbia, the Stock Exchange closing and the German declaration of war on Russia, the threat of a war became more topical. It was becoming obvious that there was no controlling the international situation. Even the weekly paper was showing concern. What few in Hull knew was that one of their own was in prison in Germany, convicted of spying for Britain. In November 1911 he had been sentenced to seven years' imprisonment with his release set at 2.10 pm on 13 June 1918.

A patriotic postcard sent by a local resident.

The leader for 2 August was entitled 'The War Cloud'. 'Not for very many years has such a danger threatened Europe as that which exists today. The crisis, intensified by the crime of Sarajevo…led to an ultimatum against the monarchy, of tolerating apology for crime, and of an indirect share in the recent murders. The confessions of the criminals show, it is stated, that the assassinations were hatched in Belgrade, that the arms and explosives were given to the murderers by Serbian officers. As a result of Austrian dissatisfaction with Serbian replies the frontier was crossed and Belgrade bombarded. As we write comes the news that a state of martial law is proclaimed in Germany, that the London Stock Exchange is closed until further notice and that the Bank Rate has been raised to 8%.'

However, while reporting this, the paper devoted the same amount of space to Irish gun-running and a clash between Nationalists and the British Army. An opinion expressed in the paper summed up what most people thought – there would be no war. 'Germany will not put her head into the noose that is ready for her. Russia on the east, France on the south-west and Great Britain in command of the North Sea.' The opposition would be so great that the Kaiser would be 'the first to cry "Peace".'

Many Germans living in Britain thought otherwise and quietly returned home. At 11 pm on 4 August Britain found itself at war. The next day the *Eastern Daily News* told its readers that 'the die is cast. Great Britain and Germany are in a state of war. That war is not of our seeking. England enters in the fray armed with the knowledge that her quarrel is a just one.'

Hull was a major export route for German ports, with German shipping agents and boats in Hull and vice versa. The sudden turn of events caught them unprepared, as the *Hull Times* reported. 'There was plenty of excitement everywhere in Hull this morning, and the German shipping offices were in a state of semi-alarm. At one office a number of German clerks were inquiring about a passage home. The last boat had gone. The agency had received a cable from Bremen that the German Army had crossed the French frontier.'

They had not been recalled and were stranded like thousands of other Germans. The French gymnasts performing at the Tivoli Music Hall were in the same position; however, they would be able to get home when recalled.

The Hull-raised East Riding Royal Engineers at camp. As a non-infantry territorial unit they are using the Lee Metford, an obsolete rifle. They would be issued the Lee Enfield for active service.

Only days before, local Germans had been respectable neighbours, now they were the enemy, even those who were naturalised or who had been born in Hull. Charles Hohenrein was a respected pork butcher. Although the family originated from Germany, they had become naturalised citizens and had children who were born in Hull. The name was a problem and made them a target. The day after the war was declared, two men, Victor Parker and Joseph Connell, broke a plate-glass window in the shop. Tried and found guilty, although it was acknowledged it may have been a spur of the moment action, the judge imposed a fine because he did not wish to stop them enlisting, which was their declared intention at the time.

Rumour abounded along with the confusion. It was reported at the docks that a newly-arrived skipper reported seeing British and French warships and submarines lined up along the German coast around Kiel. The *Hull Times* contained what it said was a tragic report; the commander of the German forces besieging Liège had died and officers and men were throwing themselves into the River Meuse because they were demoralised. In fact, the commander did not die until over a year later.

With rumour came panic buying. There was a rush to buy flour. 'Housewives were gathered together inside and outside the grocers' shops' and shopkeepers did their best to supply their customers, but supplies were limited to one stone per person. Prices rose and suddenly the flour cost 2d a stone more. Mills were besieged and millers worked flat out to meet demand. Even the news that the United States would make up any shortfall, that the UK harvest was heavy and early and that there would be no famine if war broke out, made little difference.

While the government gave the positive spin about five months' supply being harvested and that most imported food did not come from the enemy, this was not the case for some other staples. A problem with milk supplies was likely over the winter because much of the feeding stuff was imported. There were sufficient supplies of potatoes and many other foodstuffs; the issue was the purchasing power of the sovereign. By comparing 1905 prices with immediate war prices it is easy to see there was an issue for many people.

Foodstuff (weight not specified)	1905 price	1914 war price
Potatoes	13s 8d	20s
Bacon	15s 2d	20s
Bread	17s 4d	20s
English Beef	18s 3d	20s
English Mutton	18s 10d	20s
Milk	18s 3d	20s
Eggs	17s 7d	20s

Not everything went up in price. The British Gas Light Company informed customers of a price drop in coke. On and after 17 August it would cost 7d per cwt at their works and 9d if delivered.

The war was good for business and the big employers received large contracts from the government who needed supplies in previously unheard of quantities. Only days after the declaration of war, Smith & Nephew was given its biggest ever contract. In five months they supplied surgical and field dressings worth £350,000 to the government. This was followed by a Belgian contract. When the country was all but over-run, it lost all its medical supplies. Soon afterwards, Smith & Nephew was approached to provide what was needed. There was no problem with the manufacturing of the materials

One of the many trawlers requisitioned by the Royal Navy for minesweeping work. The greater part of the Hull fleet was involved in mine clearance during the war.

but there was with the time in which it was needed. The request was received on a Saturday and first supplies were needed on Monday. The whole firm were called in, and, working night and day without a break, they made dressings. 'On Monday morning they went home whilst ten tons of dressings were loaded into two special trucks attached to the 9.30 am express to London and then to Dover. They were with the Belgian authorities by 8 pm' that evening and 'as a result the company retained its Belgian contract for the remainder of the war.' The contract with the 'Serbian army was not so successful. It reached Belgrade at the same time as the city fell.' All the supplies were captured and used by the enemy.

The navy and army made preparations for a war. An essential part of this was a voluntary press blackout on naval and military movements. Readers of the *Hull Times* were informed that they would not publish 'the many particulars of unprecedented Naval and Military activity' that were occurring locally and across the country, in order to prevent information being divulged to potential enemies.

In contrast to their stated intent, which was framed to emphasise its importance, there were two pieces about troop movements. Presumably

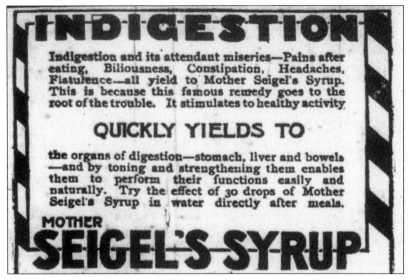

Although there was much anti-German sentiment, Mother Seigel's syrup was sold throughout the war.

any enemy spy reading the statement would read no further, or was it meant to frighten the enemy into inactivity? I have included them to show what the spy might have learned. 'During Thursday morning a detachment said to be nearly 800 strong, of soldiers of the East Yorkshire Regiment, arrived at Killingholme to protect the thirty-six huge oil tanks. The regiment is camped in the vicinity, and every inch of the immense area is closely guarded by men, fully armed, even the little wayside station adjacent to the oil fuel depot having men stationed there with fixed bayonets. Every stranger is warned off. The same close protection is observed at the Admiralty wireless station at Waltham four miles from Grimsby.' That it was not read by all is evidenced by a story later in the year.

Other stories included the German troop movements in France, the cabinet meeting to discuss the situation and a potential war zone map which was probably helpful to many. It was the Bank Holiday and many people would have time off work but would be unable to travel far because the rail excursions had been cancelled. With good weather predicted, it was a time to be outdoors. Fishing expert Waltonian

Business as usual. An advert for the necessities of life for the new soldier.

informed anglers that it should be good for fishing and that the most interesting local event would be the annual members' match of the Hull and District Amalgamated Anglers' Association at Ferriby Sluice with a prize fund of over £32. Importantly, the weeds in the Aacholme between the sluice and Saxby Bridge had been cut.

At Hornsea, West Riding troops left by special train, just a day into their summer camp. In Hull the newly arrived home 4th East Yorkshire Regiment received orders to return to barracks for orders. Hull trawlers were ordered home and vessels stayed in berth. With both sides detaining ships, goods were sitting in foreign harbours. The Wilson Liner *Castro*, with a large quantity of sugar aboard, was in Hamburg; a sugar shortage was predicted. There was a similar shortage of fruit because a considerable amount came from Hamburg.

Even before war had been declared, reservists had been called up. Among the first were naval reservists who signed on at the shipping office in Posterngate, with all their belongings in a kit-bag and some accompanied by anxious women. Hundreds of army reservists left Hull, by train, for their depots around the country. At the station the crowds were so great that the gates were closed to keep them out. As they left, Her Majesty the Queen appealed for garments for those in the services.

The President of the Women's Guild in Hull, Julia Sheffield, asked for articles to be sent to her Vice-Presidents so they could be passed on. Later in the year she thanked the people of Hull for their contribution.

A week later, the *Hull Times* carried local and further international stories, a pattern repeated throughout the war. Although the population of Hull knew about the declaration through special editions of the *Hull Daily Mail* printed just after midnight, readers were informed that England and Germany were at war, the German Army was marching through France, Liege was being violently assaulted and that Britain had mobilised.

The good news was that the bank rate had dropped from 10 to 6 per cent and that a National Relief Fund had been set up to assist groups like transport workers whose livelihood was hit by the crippled state of the shipping trade. How hard they were hit is shown by the timber shortage in August. This was the height

At the start of the war many Hull men were serving in the army. This is Charles Bogg in 1910 just before he enlisted in the 2nd East Yorkshire Regiment.

of the wood season and there was not a single ship in Victoria Dock – a sight never seen before. In Alexandra Dock, two boats had small quantities of mining timber and spars and in Town Dock one had some flooring. Over a million loads had arrived in 1913 compared with 320,000 in 1914.

Distribution of war relief commenced on 21 August; it was not only dock workers who needed help. Outside Central Hall a crowd of several hundred, mostly men, were formed into a queue by the police. Between 1,000 and 1,200 applicants had been selected for relief at this venue. In total over 4,500 were selected across Hull. Not all who applied received relief, as some 800 proved to be undeserving. Not all of those found deserving proved to be so on investigation. For falsely claiming from the fund, Frederick Kemp of 4 Marion's Crescent, a dock labourer in employment, was given twenty-one days' detention.

Like the docks, schools were quickly affected by the war due to a shortage of teachers. Many enlisted or were called up, which would affect their period of service for a pension. Hull Board of Education agreed to allow them to count the period under arms as service for superannuation and as part of the seven years needed to work in approved schools.

As a nautical city, more space was devoted to happenings on water than was the case with towns inland. This included news of Hull-registered shipping and sea news in general. Initially much was made of captured ships like the three-masted, 223-ton schooner *Else*, which had been towed into Falmouth, and 1,250-ton steamer *Wilhelm Behrens,* sailing from Rostock, that had been captured by a cruiser and taken to Glasgow.

The National Relief Fund was followed by a Belgian Relief Fund to help rebuild that country and provide for their citizens now resident in the UK. The residents of Victoria Avenue set up a home for Belgian refugee families and liaised with the Belgian Refugee committee which had been set up on 7 September with headquarters in Bowalley Lane. Eventually it would have 500 helpers, of whom 400 were women.

How had Hull been affected by just a few days of war? The local mobilisation had proceeded at a rapid rate and with great smoothness. However, business and industry had been badly affected. The papers reported that shipping was lying in every dock, coal hoists were idle and that nothing prospered except what dealt directly with the war. However, any company involved with catering and provisioning flourished and employees were working night and day to meet demand.

A real problem was the shortage of money caused by banks closing. This was quickly solved by the Bank of England. Bank notes for ten shillings and one pound were suddenly issued, exchangeable at the Bank of England for gold. Postal Orders became legal tender and banks were given powers to disallow the withdrawal of gold for hoarding, but cash would be available for wages and salaries and the normal cash requirements of daily life.

The shortage of gold was used by one jeweller as a way of selling his stock. Whether Mr Ruler of Beverley Road went abroad as his advert said is unclear, but regardless he wanted to sell his stock, giving customers 22ct gold wedding rings at 7 per cent of their value and a diamond cluster ring at ten instead of fifteen guineas.

Bank re-opening was expected to be accompanied by a rush to withdraw, so the Bank of England provided banks with extra funds for

Having just gone to camp, the territorials were recalled when hostilities were imminent.

such an occurrence, wiring The Hull Savings Bank £50,000. Some banks experienced withdrawals but not the HSB, which noted that when they re-opened 'there was nothing in the nature of a "rush". Depositors who had got unduly anxious presented themselves at the doors in George Street and when the pressure became too great for the augmented staff to cope with, two policemen – a sergeant and a constable – formed them into a queue three or four deep along the pavement in Smeaton Street, where they patiently waited until their turn came...The waiting crowd rarely exceeded 150, although at one or two periods it suddenly swelled to between 200/300. Most of the applicants received their withdrawals in paper money. There was nothing approaching the demand that had been provided for, the more sensible of the public having apparently taken to heart the warnings of the government against hoarding money unnecessarily.'

It was obvious to all that they were entering a period of change; food shortages, paper money and who knew what else? One Hull journalist suggested that perhaps women would be called upon to act as tram conductors as they were doing in St Petersburg.

Further changes and more governmental control arrived with the passing of what became known as DORA, the *Defence of the Realm Act*, on 8 August. It gave the government wide-ranging powers during the war period, such as the power to requisition buildings or land needed for the war effort, or to make regulations creating criminal offences. It would have far-reaching effects and affect everyone. The Act was amended during the war with some aspects of it remaining law well after the war was over, for example, pub opening hours during the day.

DORA covered all aspects of life: no-one was allowed to talk about naval or military matters in public places; no-one was allowed to spread rumours about military matters; no-one was allowed to buy binoculars; no-one was allowed to trespass on railway lines or bridges; no-one was allowed to melt down gold or silver; no-one was allowed to light bonfires or fireworks; no-one was allowed to give bread to horses, horses or chickens; no-one was allowed to use invisible ink when writing abroad; no-one was allowed to buy brandy or whisky in a railway refreshment room. The government could take over land, factories and workshops, censor newspapers and prosecute civilians breaking the laws. The introduction of British Summer Time caused some issues but was generally seen as a positive measure. On the other hand, restrictions on drinking raised far more objections: opening hours were cut, you could not buy a drink for someone else except with a meal – the 'no-treating' regulation – and the beer was watered down. The first person to be arrested under DORA was the revolutionary socialist John MacLean, on 27 October 1915.

One certain change would be the reduction in the number of men available for work. Since the declaration of war, the recruiting office in Pryme Street had been besieged with applicants. On more than one occasion the police were called to clear the pavement and preserve order. The recruiting officers were so busy that no one knew just how many men had enlisted, although it was accepted that it ran into a few hundreds. This first rush of men were mostly strong, 'well-built men, mostly of the artisan class', with some clerks and other business men. Even men as old as sixty were attempting to enlist but were rejected.

Hull's women mobilised almost as quickly as the men. The *Hull Times* delicately described how they were helping. 'Women who can knit, women who can sew, women who can cut out for others to sew, women who can do ambulance work, who can make bandages, who can cook for individuals – are all busy, for this is not the time for the folding up of talents in a napkin.'

At the same time councils in the area, realising that the conflict would result in many wounded, offered accommodation. Cottingham and Hornsea were quick to offer and this was followed by Hull Corporation offering the new Workhouse Hospital with 240 beds. The Hull Hairdresser's Association made a kind offer to help the wounded. They were prepared to attend the temporary hospitals for the purposes of shaving and hairdressing.

The first wounded would be regular soldiers who would eventually be replaced by the volunteers. In order to provide replacements more rapidly, territorial units (Terriers) were asked to volunteer for overseas service. The 4th East Yorkshire Regiment was asked, and Colonel How, fifteen officers and eighty-four per cent of the men volunteered.

This call-up of reservists and embodiment of the Terriers had an immediate effect on local industry. Blundell, Spence and Co. were concerned about future employment and short time but wanted to help its employees. For salaried employees, posts were held open and wives and families liberally assisted. For those on weekly wages, a form had to be completed detailing their present rank and daily pay, any extra payments, the amount allowed for their wife and amount for any children and the number of children. With this information Blundell's, for those on 1s a day, brought the government allowance up to 14s a week with 4s 6d for each child. For men paid over 1s a day, the difference was deducted from the Blundell's allowance.

Hull was not immune to seeing spies everywhere or to skittish sentries firing their rifles. Thomas Pearson Taylor, aged twenty-three, on a visit to Saltburn, failed to answer the challenges of a sentry on the promenade shortly before midnight on 21 August and was shot through the chest and died soon afterwards. Riding a motorcycle, he did not hear the sentry. He was the son of Alderman Taylor of Hull.

Four alleged spies at Paull were charged under the Official Secrets Act. One was a Russian Jew, another a Norwegian, and the other two were from Hull, one being a naval architect. They had travelled from Hull on motorbikes and passed through the line of defences when they were stopped by armed sentries. They were discharged, but the paper warned readers that they were just as likely to be shot as locked up if they did this.

Spy paranoia was accompanied by anti-German sentiment. This started quietly with window signs and grew into attacks on shops. At first it was a simple request to shop-keepers: 'No more German or Austrian goods will be stocked in this shop so long as similar British and goods of friendly nations can be obtained.'

The Magistrates Bench continued to be busy with the usual and some more unusual cases – there *was* a war on. Typical and atypical charges included Eleanor Hornigold being found guilty of being drunk and disorderly and with assaulting two police officers. She was let off on the first charge but given five weeks' imprisonment for biting an officer's right arm. Frederick Atkins was remanded while the Admiralty replied to the charge of him deserting HMS *Bachante*. More unusual was the case of the Chinese aliens. Gong Wing Sing, Gong Yuke Brew, Sing Lee, Wong Sue, Wong Yuen, Ham Owen and Chang Denchow were charged with failing to report themselves under the Alien Act. As they could not speak or understand English, they could not understand the procedure so were allowed their liberty on their own recognisance.

In order to reduce the number of military personnel appearing before the bench, like Eleanor Hornigold, the military authorities took steps to prevent this. All licensees in Hull and district were told by the Humber District authorities that they could only serve members of the forces between 7 and 9 pm.

How effective this restriction was initially is shown by a comment in the *Hull Daily Mail* on 14 September. 'Despite the fact that public-houses were closed in Hull on Saturday night at nine o'clock with accordance of the recent order, there were nearly twenty cases of drunkenness heard at the Police Court on Monday.'

For many men, health or work and family commitments stopped them enlisting. There were many other ways in which they could help the war effort; volunteering with St John's was one.

Regardless of the war situation, the cricket results remained essential reading. In the second week of the war, in the late war news, Yorkshire were 231 for 4, rain stopped play between Essex and Gloucestershire, Derbyshire were 28 for 0, Hampshire were all out for 323 and Lancashire were 131 all out. The latest war news was that 400,000 Austrians had been repulsed along the Serbian frontier.

With two first class rugby teams and a football team, reports of their games were also essential reading. Sometimes they even appeared as comments in soldiers' or sailors' letters, like that from C. Harvey serving on HMS *Lydiard* with the Harwich Force just after he had been in action at the Battle of the Heligoland Bight. 'Just a line to let you know that we have at last had an innings at the Germans, and, my, it was a go; fully seven hours we fought shot for shot. I had the greatest pleasure in seeing four German ships go down. We never knew but that it might be our turn next, as great shells were falling all around us... we hope the Tiger's centre-forward shoots better than the Germans shot at us or Hull City will be at the bottom.'

The four ships sunk were V187, a V180 class destroyer; *Ariadne*, a Gazelle class light cruiser; *Cöln*, a Kolberg class light cruiser and *Mainz*, a Kolberg class light cruiser. Harvey's ship had sunk the *Mainz*.

Enlistment slowed down but it was boosted by increasing the upper age limit. On one day, 28 August, 144 enlisted. At Wenlock Barracks, sixty men were passed as fit on 28 August. Most men volunteered for the infantry, with the 4th East Yorkshires being a popular choice. This was not the only enlistment office. Men were also being attested at City Hall, Pryme Street and the Royal Army Medical Corps (RAMC) HQ in Walton Street.

Some were rejected because of insufficient chest expansion. Mr. Frank Tubb, gymnastic trainer, of the Young Peoples' Institute, offered them assistance. All many needed was a fortnight's workout with him. He offered his services free to all who could be accommodated in the gym.

It was not long before enlistment rolls of honour started to appear. An early one was that of Messrs Croft & Son of Hull. It displayed the names of the members of staff who voluntarily enlisted and was exhibited in their Beverley Road, Witham and Anlaby establishments.

The creation of 'Pals' battalions also helped boost recruitment. The *Hull Times* reported this phenomenon. 'Lord Kitchener's second

Territorial units went to their war stations when hostilities started. These were often many miles from their home area. Watched by passers-by, these men of the Lancashire Fusiliers are training in a Hull street.

100,000 men have been obtained, and the third 100,000 are well on the way. In London 4,000 to 5,000 recruits have been signed on daily, and in nearly every big town commercial and "pals" battalions, of men of the same occupations, have all been in vogue. Hull is doing its share: the 4th East Yorkshires are going on Foreign Service, and a Commercial Battalion is being raised.' A further increase in numbers was expected when the harvest was fully in.

The 'pals' were first mentioned on 31 August and were to be followed by three further battalions. Recruitment began at 10 am on 1 September at Wenlock Barracks. Enlistment was brisk and within a few days the battalion was at strength. Military service and war go hand-in-hand with death; preferably a hero's death on active service abroad. This was not to be the case for a number of recruits. One of the last to enlist was the first to die. Private Adams was buried in Western Cemetery, with full military honours, on 19 September after succumbing to brain fever. Before joining-up he had lived with his widowed mother at 3, Lily Grove. He was formerly a painter with Messrs Goddard, Walker & Brown. Within five days of his death on 18 September the battalion suffered another death – Sergeant Gardiner.

Hull was not only forming infantry units. On 7 September the 1st Hull Heavy Battery and Ammunition Column was authorised and formed, solely of Hull men with previous experience, by the local Territorial Force (TF). Its guns arrived in late October by rail to the goods station in Kingston Street and were taken over by the 200 strong battery under the command of Captain J. C. Williams, RNR. The 4.7 inch guns were dragged along the streets to Wenlock Barracks before being transferred to their HQ on Holderness Road. After training and renaming as 11th Hull Heavy Battery, it sailed in January 1916 to fight in East Africa.

On the same day the 1st Hull Heavy Battery was forming, recruits were coming forward for the second 'Pals' battalion. After a meeting on 7 September, 'a steady stream of strong, intelligent, and healthy looking young men came forward offering their services for their King and country. The 7th Battalion East Yorks having become "full up", a further battalion is being formed which it is expected will be complete by the end of the present week. Yesterday no less than 312 recruited at the City Hall. At 11 o'clock this morning the number towards the 8th

Musicians before the start of a recruiting parade outside the West Park photographic studio.

Battalion was increased to 340.' The men were enlisting voluntarily and all the staff involved in their processing, from clerks to doctors, also gave their time freely.

So successful were the campaigns to raise these units that further Hull battalions were raised. The Commercials had been followed by the Tradesmen, mentioned above, the Sportsmen – enlistment started on 14 September – and then T'Others.

This fourth battalion, and a second Heavy Battery, were sanctioned by Lord Kitchener with recruiting for both to start on 16 November. Lord Nunburnholme again appealed to their pride. The purpose of a fourth battalion was partly civic pride, as it would put Hull on a par with cities like Liverpool, Manchester and Newcastle, which had each raised a brigade. 'It is to be hoped that the young men of Hull will promptly rise to the occasion and that "The Boys of the Hull Brigade" will very shortly be ready to fight shoulder to shoulder with their comrades in arms in support of our hard-pressed but victorious troops at the front.'

All were formed into a brigade and would fight together until disbanded through a shortage of men in 1918. With many under height men wanting to enlist, a Bantam Battalion was formed. The 5th, or 'Reserve', Battalion raised was largely composed of men of smaller stature. These men were known as 'Bantams', little men with big hearts! This fine Battalion was also known as 'Lord Roberts' (Bob's) Battalion'. Unfortunately it did not reach full strength and the men were used as reserves for the other battalions.

The focus of Hull's military participation has always centred on the 'Pals' at the expense of other units which many Hull men joined. Scant thought is given to a battalion that was raised in Hull at the same time – 17th Battalion Northumberland Fusiliers. Originally an infantry battalion, it became a Pioneer Battalion in 1915, serving with distinction on the Western Front.

On 8 September the North Eastern Railway issued a circular calling on men who wished to serve together to fill it in and return it. Like many of the bigger employers, the company was 'prepared to make adequate provision for wives, families and dependents; to keep men's positions open for them; to pay their contributions to Superannuation and Pension Funds, and to provide accommodation for the families of men who were occupying company's houses.' The response was far

Some of Hull's Jewish volunteers. Most are in civilian attire but the armband shows that they have joined one of the Hull battalions.

Newly-enlisted members of the 1st Hull Battalion. Their style of dress clearly indicates that they were mostly office workers. Note the two 'wags' in the front row with their caps reversed.

Measuring the height of the first member of the Hull City Battalion.

a/O.R.S. Thorlander № 1.

1st HULL BATTALION
The East Yorkshire Regiment.

STANDING ORDERS.
MISCELLANEOUS.

King's Regulations and Standing Orders.—All ranks are to make themselves acquainted with Extracts from King's Regulations issued October 1914, and with these Standing Orders. Company Commanders will have a copy of each issued to all Officers and others joining.

Venereal Disease.—All men becoming affected with venereal disease to report sick without delay.

Smoking.—Cigarettes are prohibited on all duties and fatigues and during the whole time men are out of barracks on marches or for training

Dogs and Animals.—Are prohibited unless a permit is previously obtained from the Adjutant.

Hawkers.—No edibles or drinkables are to be purchased from hawkers within half a mile of barracks, &c., or during marches, manoeuvres, training or work.

No longer civilians, the newly-enlisted 1st Hull Battalion were now subject to military regulations. The first Standing Orders for the men were simple.

greater than anticipated, with 3,000 indicating a wish to join a battalion that needed 1,100. Recruiting commenced on 14 September. Minimum height was 5 feet 6 inches and minimum chest size was 35½ inches. Within a few days, the battalion was up to strength. They would be accommodated in two large warehouses on King George Dock provided by the Hull and Barnsley Railway. For the next two months they were a regular sight around the area. Then suddenly they were moved to Patrington.

How effective was the enlistment campaign in Hull? The following enlistment table, provided in the *Hull Times*, compares recruitment in some of the larger cities in the country but gives no date/time parameters.

City	Population	Recruits
Birmingham	840,000	25,000
Glasgow	785,000	23,000
Liverpool	747,000	19,000
Manchester	715,000	28,000
Hull	290,000	6,000
Newcastle	267,000	15,000
Cardiff	183,000	11,000

William Barton wanted to join the army or Red Cross but was told by the magistrate that he was not suitable. The reason for turning down an able-bodied man was simple. He was deaf and dumb and had appeared before the Bench seventeen times before. This time it was for being drunk and disorderly and head-butting pedestrians. In custody, he was violent and tried to kick and bite the arresting officer and behaved like a mad man on the way to the police station. He was fined 10s plus costs or in default, fourteen days with hard labour.

As in other areas, there was an unspoken competition to see who could claim to have the most sons serving. By late October, Mrs Parker, a widow living at 67 Bean Street, had four at the front: William with the Royal Naval Division, Anthony with the West Yorkshires, Jack with 1st Lincolns and Fred with the Royal Garrison Artillery (RGA), and also two in training, Walter serving with 3rd East Yorkshires and Thomas with 4th East Yorkshires.

How liberal Hull was is shown by the postponement of a military event of some importance. A recruiting march, designed to highlight the newly-formed Hull Battalions, that was to have been held on a Sunday so that it did not clash with other events, was cancelled after opposition from strict Sabbatarian Quakers who wanted Sunday respected.

To help boost recruitment and explain why Britain was fighting, Lord Curzon, who was to become a member of the coalition government in 1915, spoke at town halls across the land. In Reading, the paper said he gave a masterly oration to a packed hall while the *Hull Times* that he gave 'a masterly survey of the situation, and made an unanswerable plea for national service.' He told the audience that it would be a long war because 'we have to turn the Germans out of

An advert from the Hull Times asking for sportsmen to join the newly-formed 3rd Hull Battalion.

An appeal from the government for more men to join the army – not that this was needed in Hull. By the end of the year Hull had raised at least seven battalions of infantry.

Hull's second territorial battalion, the cyclists, were mobilised and sent to their war station. Before they could leave they had to go round the city requisitioning bikes because they did not have enough.

Belgium, to turn them out of France…and town by town, fort by fort, city by city, to defeat and subjugate them in their own country.' A month later he said he was shocked of talk about it being over by Christmas and predicted that it would be 'more than one Christmas before the soldiers returned.'

All these men needed more space for training purposes. For this the Humber Defence General Officer Commanding (GOC) had requested use of all Hull's available space, including the fairground. There may have been a war on, but the Corporation decided that it would hold the annual fair regardless.

Just a month into the war came the first Hull casualty. Captain Travis-Cook, son of Lieutenant Colonel Travis-Cook of Hull, was severely wounded fighting in the streets of Mons. Serving with the South Lancashire Regiment, he was leading a bayonet charge when a bullet went through his neck and down his spine, coming out in the lower part of his back. Shortly after this the first wounded enlisted man was named as Corporal John Shaw of the Royal Engineers, who was recovering at home in Ella Street with a bullet wound in his shoulder. He had only been married a month and a day when he was recalled. Some, such as Private J.R. Gardiner, a twenty-three-year-old in the Coldstream Guards, managed to write home about their experiences. Wounded in the wrist on 6 September, he proudly informed his mother that he had killed more than three Germans and that, while he lay wounded, the shells were falling just yards away – and that his feet were sore from marching 220 miles in just six days.

It was not long before the first deaths. Cottingham-born thirty-year-old Private Albert Teasdale, a reservist in the Coldstream Guards, was killed on 9 September. A bricklayer with Bilton the builder, he lived at 68 Raglan Street with his wife and two children aged four and two. His widow received an official communication after his death. 'The King commands me to assure you of the true sympathy of His Majesty and the Queen in your sorrow.' The widow of Driver H. Hammond – Royal Field Artillery – of 4 Worthing Street also received this communication. Although working for the North Eastern Railway he was recalled and was killed in action on 12 September. Soon the isolated stories turned into casualty lists.

With winter rapidly approaching, the previous appeal for garments was extended. The East Riding Territorial Force (ERTF) requested

Officers and NCOs of the 17th Northumberland Fusiliers pose for their photograph on King George Dock.

*The 17th Northumberland
Fusiliers were raised in
Hull and trained on the
docks.*

winter underclothing and other articles in large numbers all to be sent to Lady Nunburnholme who was heading the appeal. How they worked out that they needed 7,000 grey flannel shirts, 7,000 pairs of worsted socks, 3,500 cardigan jackets but only 2,000 pairs of woollen pants was not explained. The sizes requested show how much taller we are 100 years on. Sixty per cent of all the clothing was for men between 5ft 4in to 5ft 7in, thirty-five per cent was for between 5ft 7in and 5ft 10in; presumably the unaccounted five per cent was for taller men.

Lady Nunburnholme also set up the Voluntary Aid Committee in Hull, headquarters at Peel House, 150 Spring Bank. This distributed clothing to soldiers at the front as well as training nurses and providing hospital accommodation for troops in Hull. It also sent parcels to PoWs.

Hull men were now serving all over the country as well as at the front. The ERTF request did not cover most of these who had to rely on friends and relatives to send them extra clothing. One enterprising commanding officer went to the local papers to ask for their help. Captain McLaren asked for people to send blankets and warm clothing for the 162 men from Hull who were serving in the Army Service Corps (ASC) Company attached to the York and Durham Infantry Brigade near Darlington.

Being a gateway city for emigrants, there were many Germans and some Austrians living in the vicinity. At the start of the war, German waiters in Hornsea had been detained, but most reported to the police and got on with their lives. The situation changed during October when 160 were arrested and detained aboard the SS *Borodino* before being handed over to the military authorities. This was followed by non-naturalised German and Austrian residents of military age – eighteen to thirty-five – being taken into custody. After visits from friends, they were taken to Wakefield.

Not all had been compliant. Paul Neubach was arrested and sentenced to six months' imprisonment for having failed to comply with the Alien Registration Order. The fact that he had served in the British Army meant nothing to the Bench.

Another foreigner, a Dane, also fell foul of the law. He was given two months in prison for failing to notify the police of his change of address. The man had just returned from sea to find that his landlady had moved and not registered his change.

Along with constant need for more men for the colours, warm articles for those at the front or in training, was a need for money. This was collected in many ways, subscriptions, donations, flag days, collections: auctions; any way that money could be raised was tried. Hospital Sunday, 25 October, was a collection day and citizens were urged to dig deep to help maintain Hull's voluntary hospitals which, with winter coming, would find their resources sorely stretched. In response to this, Fenner's offered to give £500 if £1,500 could be raised elsewhere. As only £1,000 had been raised, the mayor asked for financial assistance to reach this total.

At the same time the *Hull Daily Mail* set up its own fund. It wanted, apart from contributions, cardigan jackets and sweaters, mufflers, body belts, woollen blankets and balaclava caps and socks – the same as other requests, but with a difference; each garment would have the donor's name stitched into it. People wanting anonymity

One of the first local officers to be killed was Captain Twiss of the Royal Engineers. He died in Mesopotamia and is buried in Basra.

had a little message attached, 'From a friend'. Every article would go to a Hull man and all articles were to be purchased locally.

Men in uniform, when not on duty, tended to get bored. In order to stop any problems and out of kindness, Beverley Road Baths was converted into a soldiers' club. Its size is shown by the number who attended its opening – two thousand. In the games room, soldiers could play bagatelle, billiards and darts among the many choices of games available. The large hall was used as a supper bar and recreation room, while a third room provided space for reading and writing, a room where silence had to be observed. There were no issues with smoking, which was allowed all over the building. 'Tobacco, cigars and cigarettes, as well as tea, coffee, mineral waters, meat pies and every delicacy imaginable could be obtained from the buffet at popular prices.' In the reading room there was a Post Office for stamps, postal orders and so on. A library provided books, papers and periodicals. For 1d, the men could use the slipper baths if they had their own towel and soap, or 2d if they had to be provided.

As a maritime city, Hull's population was spread across the oceans, resulting in stories about boats at sea and men far away from home. In the North Sea, the trawler *St Lawrence* was reported missing during October. Although it was a Grimsby boat, the skipper, Henry Fletcher and the mate, John Pawlett, were both Hull men. At the same time another Grimsby boat made the *Hull Times*, again because of its Hull connection. This time it was about a murder. At Milford Haven, J. Kavanagh, the Hull-born 2nd engineer on the steam trawler *Queenstown*, was charged with wilful murder. He had stabbed the steward in the neck during an argument.

In common with weekly papers across the country, the *Hull Times* published snippets about the men at the front, telling of under-age soldiers, how the men felt about their task, about the wounded and the dead. When recruiters knew that the lower age limit was eighteen, would they believe a sixteen-year-old or why would parents let an under-age son enlist? However, this happened regularly. Mr and Mrs Mussett of 77 Grange Street, obviously had no problem with their sixteen-year-old son serving. It was noted that Private R. Mussett of the RAMC was serving in France with 11th Stationary Hospital. The same issue told readers about Private Broughton, of 15 Clara's Terrace, a reservist at the front with the 1st East Yorkshires. He had been wounded seven times and was recovering in England. He had also been shot through the hat five times. Sergeant Pashley of 13 Arthur's Terrace, a twenty-five year-old regular with the 1st Lincolnshires, wrote home expressing how he felt. His father was dead and he was an only son. 'Dear Mother' he wrote, 'I am for the front, and am quite willing to be shot. If I am shot I know I shall have done my duty to my King and country.' Even in death those from a higher station in life were generally given more space in the papers – but not always. While recording the death of the Earl of Durham's youngest brother at the front, it also noted the death of a 'brave Hull soldier', Gunner Frank Wilkinson, and accorded him a photo and the same column space.

How much information was sometimes provided seems strange to modern eyes. Would you want the whole population of Hull to know that your son had died of a gunshot wound through the lung and that he had also lost the thumb and forefinger of his left hand and been shot through the right arm? The parents of Francis Lloyd of 14 Bates Terrace obviously didn't object to this appearing in the papers.

Families often provided the papers with photographs of their loved ones when they were missing, wounded, ill or dead. Twenty-year-old Able Seaman John Merriken of 2 Palm Grove, Hessle Road and twenty-five-year-old Leading Stoker Charles Poulsen of 17 Lorne Avenue were both killed on 26 November. The ship they were serving on, HMS Bulwark, *a pre-dreadnought battleship, internally exploded at Sheerness.*

Mention has previously been made of the hope of recruiting more men when the harvest was in. Martinmas was another period when the army hoped men would enlist. 9 November was traditionally Martinmas hiring day, when agricultural workers could move from one farm, usually with a financial incentive, to another. In order to attract the healthy, outdoor men, the villages and towns were filled with military march-outs, processions and military bands. As many of the men came into town for the holiday and visited the hostelries, recruiting was good for a short period.

In Hull, a second recruiting campaign commenced with varying day-by-day results. On the first day 377 men enlisted at City Hall, the next day only 146, followed by daily enlistment totals of 111, 84, 49, 110, 123, 87, 41, 42 and 45. In total only 1,215 enlisted, the bulk for the 4th Hull Pals (870) with a further 24 the next day. The new 2nd Heavy Battery managed just six men on 27 November. As in other parts of the country, there was competition between the services. The Royal Navy were recruiting for skilled personnel.

With the approach of Christmas, Princess Mary decided to provide serving sailors and soldiers with a gift. Lord Devonshire appealed in the *Hull Times* for subscriptions to the fund. The gift was to consist of a brass embossed tobacco box, a pipe, a tinder lighter, tobacco and cigarettes, with a special version for Indian troops and non-smokers. Hull of course gave generously.

Everyone was after money. Lady Nunburnholme politely asked for help which equated to a donation. She asked readers if they could help her send unbleached calico bandages to the Lady Sykes Hospital in Malo-les-Bains, preferably 3in and 6in wide, because they were using thousands of them to help the wounded.

At the start of the war there had been a shortage of flour, the price of which went up by 1s a sack around Christmas. As Christmas

Papers across the country included photographs of patriotic families. The patriotic Bourne family includes two sons-in-law.

A card sold across the country in memory of the fallen.

approached, there was a shortage of cattle at Hull market but less so than in 1913. Fortunately, the quality was good and there was enough for everyone for their Christmas meal. However, there was a shortage of turkey and geese in Hull, resulting in high prices. This was put down to the military and public institutions purchasing so many and the non-arrival of geese as usual from Russia.

Due to military movements, there were fewer Christmas excursions but over the Christmas period the NER offered cheap travel to the Channel Islands, Wales and Scotland and many other destinations in England for Christmas Day and Boxing Day. Obviously the military did not need the trains and no matter what the situation, business is business.

What was the first war Christmas like? 'The morning of Christmas Day was cold and frosty, and though there was a thaw during the day, the weather remained fair.' The *Hull Daily Mail* told its readers that Christmas 1914 was memorable because of the war and that the gaiety and merriment associated with the birth of the Prince of Peace was out of place.

Not everything was changed. Civic heads continued the tradition of visiting council centres. The Lord Mayor and Lady Mayoress, with the Sheriff and his wife, visited the Naval Hospital in Argyle Street. At Sculcoates Workhouse, the Mayor and his party arrived during the early afternoon. Prior to their arrival, gifts of tobacco, oranges, tea and sugar were given to the inmates. At noon they were served with 'an excellent dinner' of roast beef, roast pork, potatoes, turnips and plum puddings with sweet sauce, followed by coffee. The quantities provided were approximately 600lb of beef, 300lb of pork, 6cwt each of potatoes and turnips, 98lb of pudding and 25 gallons of sauce.

Soldiers at Newland Avenue School enjoyed a small gift. The 150 soldiers received 2,200 cigarettes, about 3lb of tobacco, cigars and numerous books of cigarette papers, match boxes and nearly 200 bars of chocolate between them. Their benefactors were the girls of the school.

In Victoria Hospital 'Christmas Day was ushered in for the 70 odd in-patients...by Santa Claus paying his visit in the early hours and leaving toys, books, clothing, etc...on the cot of every child in the hospital. The children had naturally anticipated his visit, and had carefully hung up their stockings which had been overlooked by good old Santa Claus.' During the morning they were visited by the Mayor and Sheriff with their wives.

At the Anlaby Road Workhouse, the 'Guardians and friends did their utmost to let the old people thoroughly enjoy their Christmas.' Cooking started at 4 am to get the meal ready for noon; 450 inmates consumed vast quantities of food and afterwards received, like the inmates of Sculcoates Workhouse, gifts of tobacco, tea, oranges and sugar, with sweets for the women and pipes for the men.

There were also the customary services at places of worship and, because of the war, concerts were arranged for soldiers billeted in the area. Matches on the City and Rovers' ground attracted large crowds.

The spy fear continued unabated. A German was arrested in Hampshire for asking questions about the Hull defences – as if a sergeant in the 11th Northumberland Fusiliers would know much about them. Closer to home, Archibald Cocks, who lived in a bungalow on the cliffs at Filey, was sent to Hull gaol for two months after being court-martialled. His crime was serious. He had not declared possessing a portable wireless instrument in his sitting room. He was released in under three weeks after his MP had intervened.

Some older readers may recall the vagaries of using the Humber ferry. Before the bridge it was the quickest way to Lincolnshire but one prone to cancellation – usually because of the weather, as happened on Christmas Eve 1914. A reporter from the *Hull Times* described what happened. '800 passengers bound for Lincolnshire had a very unpleasant experience on Christmas Eve', one that would make it stand out for years to come. 'Fog enveloped the Humber, making the journey to New Holland impracticable. The boat was late arriving in Hull and after landing at 10.30, the hundreds of waiting, half frozen passengers, rushed for the boat.'

Quickly the boat was filled to overflowing. For the first half hour, the more cheerful spirits sang patriotic and other songs but by 12 pm hope died and people began to make themselves as comfortable as circumstances would permit. 'Children in prams and in arms were crying. In the cabin women fainted, it had become a "black hole" for want of ventilation. People lay on the floors, invaded the engine room where they could only stay a short while and they had to go back on the frosty decks at 2 am. Others walked the streets of the Old Town. A few lively ones sang Christmas hymns in Mytongate. A few found space in unheated waiting rooms.'

By 7.45 am when it was light, the boat had been expected to leave as the fog had lifted. However, now there was a different problem – many new passengers had arrived. By 8 am there was still no movement but when a new captain arrived orders were given to cast off. To no avail though – the steering gear had frozen. The boat eventually left and arrived in New Holland just after 8.30 am where a large crowd of passengers were waiting to go to Hull.

It was generally acknowledged that crime decreased during the war, but it neither disappeared nor changed its character. The story of Louisa Turner and respectable-looking young shop assistants of previously good character typifies the type of crime that occurred before, during and after the war. Clarice Boyd, aged sixteen, and Elma Martin, aged nineteen, had systematically robbed their employer over a considerable period. In nine months they had stolen 532 pairs of boots which they gave to Turner, who sold them. They received little money and were afraid to stop because she threatened to expose them. All pleaded guilty. Turner was sentenced to six months with hard labour, while Boyd and Martin, who were described as weak, were given probation.

More married men volunteered for the army than single men. Hull was no exception.

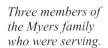

Three members of the Myers family who were serving.

THREE BROTHERS.

NO 1.—CORPORAL GEORGE MYERS, 3rd EAST YORKS., NOW AT YORK.
NO 2.—SERGEANT CHARLES MYERS, 1st. EAST YORKS., AT FRONT.
NO 3.—A. B. JAMES HUBBARD MYERS, HOME FLEET.
(ALL OF HULL).

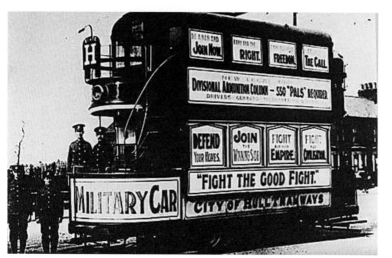

A Hull tram being used to stimulate enlistment; this time for the 32nd Divisional Ammunition Column which included a number of the city constabulary. Note the use of the term 'Pals' on the large panel.

With

Best Wishes

+ for a +

Happy Christmas

+ and a +

Victorious New Year.

From

The Princess Mary

and Friends at

+ Home +

+ + + +

The message inside the Christmas card from Princess Mary that every airman, sailor and soldier received.

For Loyalty and Freedom.

The Christmas card brought greetings and showed a family's patriotism.

For His Country's Sake.

Bereaved families sent specially designed Christmas cards that showed their grief and also their Christmas spirit.

·1914·

The front of the Christmas card every soldier received, from the Princess Mary Fund, during the Christmas period of 1914. Due to the numbers involved many did not receive theirs until well after Christmas.

The "Hull Times" Christmas Card to Our Readers.

"A MERRY CHRISTMAS TO ALL"

"AND HERE'S TO THE ABSENT ONES"

The Hull Times wished its readers, many of whom would be serving away from Hull, a Merry Christmas.

Brown's the booksellers sold thermos flasks, wallets and writing equipment as well as books.

The first man to enlist in the 1st Hull Battalion was soon promoted. This is Sergeant Tholander, enlistment number 10/1. He transferred to the Army Ordnance Corps and survived the war.

Members of the newly-formed 12th East Yorkshire Regiment, at that time known as the Third Hull Pals or The Sportsmen's Battalion. As with most newly-formed battalions, uniforms were not available so the men trained in their own clothes.

With so many men in the army, space to train was at a premium. Here some of the sportsmen's battalion train on the Hull cricket ground.

With the loss of three capital ships on the same day, numbers swelled at Newland Orphans' Home.

"HULL TIMES" LOCAL PHOTO GALLERY.

Four members of a new organisation, the Hull Naval Brigade.

Not all Hull men wanted to serve in local units. These are three who volunteered for the Northumberland Fusiliers. Private Charlton, mentioned earlier, is on the left.

CHAPTER 2

1915:
Deepening Conflict

How was the old year viewed? The papers shared their opinions with their readers. 'Nineteen hundred and fourteen has been full of sorrows – a black year, and yet not without mercies and blessings. Its end was worthy of it. It has been the wettest December for a generation.'

The year had opened with strikes in Leeds and Dublin, continued with a deadlock in Dublin and suffragette bombs but 'ended with a united nation.'

And the New Year? 'Seldom perhaps have we stepped across the threshold of a new year amidst greater portents of storm and disaster. This morning the New Year opened in bright weather, that is comparatively speaking, but already disasters have marred the day.'

The leader writer had penned his thoughts in the afternoon after he had heard of the sinking of the battleship *Formidable* in the channel and a rail smash at Ilford that killed ten and injured more than 500. Nevertheless, the paper wished its readers, far and near, a Happy New Year in all sincerity.

That the future held portents of storm and disaster is shown by a warning to the people of Hull. If bombs were

Papers across the country carried this advert on 1 January 1915.

By early 1915, the now 11th East Yorkshire Regiment (previously 2nd Hull) were fully kitted out and had moved to a camp outside Hull.

Before moving to a new camp the men of the 17th Northumberland Fusiliers were inspected by the directors of the North Eastern Railway Company.

Bomb damage after the first raid.

Five people died when 11 and 12 East Street received a direct hit.

dropped, readers were told how they should react. The London Commissioner of Police advised them 'to stay under cover, preferably in basements, upon hearing the sound of gunfire or explosives. On the street there was the danger from shell and from bullets from the guns used against hostile aircraft.' This warning was prompted by deaths in Paris. After a raid people liked to pick up fragments as souvenirs but they were advised to hand them in so the size and type of the bomb could be determined.

Hull Board of Education issued a circular on arrangements for children at school if there was an invasion, air raid or bombardment. 'The children were to be detained in school and not allowed to go home.' It was up to the Elementary Education Board to decide whether to provide dug-outs and iron-proof shelters for exposed schools. Over the Humber in Grimsby, the opposite was held to be safer; there would be less danger to them scattered than in one place. When it came to making a decision, the sub-committee followed Grimsby's lead. They overrode the Mayor's proclamation and told school heads that children living close, that is within five minutes, could go home. Those living further away could go home when collected.

Covering every base later in the year, the Lord Mayor notified the public that in case of bombardment by air, land or sea or hostile landing, civil hospitals and asylums should not fly the Red Cross flag. Hospitals, places where the sick and wounded were collected, buildings dedicated to public worship, art, science, charitable purposes or historical monuments were to be clearly marked by a large, stiff rectangular panel divided diagonally into two painted triangular portions, the upper portion black and the lower portion white. Only military and naval establishments for the sick and wounded could fly the Red Cross flag.

To help warn of an impending raid sirens were sounded. In Hull, throughout the war, there was only one hooter. It was fixed on Mill Tower at Beverley Road and was known to the town as 'Blundell's Lizzie'.

War-time regulations reduced the amount of street lighting to help combat the peril of raids. As in other towns, the darkness caused problems, especially in the dock area and particularly for those getting on and off the boats. People just disappeared, like the captain of the Norwegian vessel *Sara*. He fell into King George Dock around 1 am on 16 December and, although the water was searched by divers, he was not found.

Like most other weekly papers, the *Hull Times* described Christmas Day at the front, firstly because they had letters from a local man, secondly because people were interested, and thirdly because events there were almost incredible. A Hull officer described his day. 'After distributing Princess Mary's Christmas gifts to my company, I rode down to the trenches to have lunch with an old friend…we had two bottles of champagne between four, one goose and one tinned plum pudding…As one approached the trenches by a dug-out road the unwelcome snap of bullets from the ever intermittent sniping made one understand it was really not Whitefriargate…The Germans left some of their trenches and came over to talk with our men, and I also hear a football match has been arranged for New Year's Day.'

It is interesting that, two weeks later, the paper published a letter that contradicted the story of the truce. Perhaps it was the regiment that Private Escritt, of 49 Kimberley Street, was serving in – the Coldstream Guards – that didn't want a truce. He wrote to tell readers about his experiences. 'I have seen in the press a few letters from NCOs and men...as to how they spent Christmas Day in the trenches, and must say my own experiences were very different...we kept exchanging bullets and bombs as usual, this is the truth, and not any of those lies which are being circulated.'

For those too old, too young legally (in the same issue the *Hull Times* reported the wounding, at the front, of a fifteen-year-old soldier who had gone to France in August when he was fourteen), those who worked in what would become reserved occupations or were too unwell, there were other ways to serve. A meeting was held in the City Hall by the Chief Constable to explain the Civic Guard, Special Constabulary and the 1st Volunteer Battalion of the East Yorkshire Regiment. These para-military formations were not the first to be formed. The Hull Golfers Battalion was already 200 strong and was the first of the unofficial Home Defence Forces. The meeting was to recruit men for these units in non-combatant roles but, in the event of invasion, the Civic Guard was expected to take up arms. The aim was three battalions and until it received War Office backing it would receive funds from the East Riding Council and Hull Corporation. It soon had 2,800 rifles.

The need for money was just as pressing at the start of the year as before. This time it was Lord Nunburnholme who was asking for donations to equip the East Yorkshire Volunteer Brigade. Money raised would purchase arms and equipment for the three battalions being raised across the Riding.

The Special Constabulary assisted the police force, which had been reduced in size by the call-up of reservists. Although there were fewer police, the estimate for expenditure was £6,000 higher than 1914 – all of which would have to be met by Hull Council. The increase was due to the number of police reserves, the increased pay of the force and the number of extra duties due to Hull being a port. There was simply no way to reduce costs.

Letters from the front often described the conditions, which no doubt boosted donations to soldier-linked worthy causes, and explained why men felt they should be there. Public interest in these letters is shown by the number published. In February Private Dale, a Hull man serving with 21 Brigade, wrote to his sister. 'We are having a rough time of it now; it's a wonder how a man's constitution stands it. We are in the middle of winter and have had severe frost and snow, and afterwards a thaw, which turned the country into a quagmire. For days we have been wet through and covered from head to foot in clay…the weather is awful but we get plenty of food. Otherwise, I don't think we could stand the cold and sometimes for days without any rest or sleep. We can't sleep in the trenches, as we are drenched with rain and sleet, and up to the ankles in water. It makes you wish you were back at your own fireside again until you look at it in a proper light, and see that it's a war that must be fought and won.' This no doubt reflected the views of most of the readers.

As well as describing their life and conditions, some men predicted how long the war would last. In a letter to his wife, Trooper J. Roche of 2 Hawthorn Grove, told her that the war would last a long time, perhaps even a further year. For good measure he informed her that civilians had no idea what it was like at the front where there was nothing but mud.

As well as letters, the paper printed snippets about military life, sometimes amusing, some informative, others about amazing escapes from danger, or the inadequacy of the army and its inability to keep track of its soldiers. In the latter category came the story of Private W. Gregson, of Hodgson Street, serving with the Lincolnshire Regiment. He received an official letter informing him that he was dead, having died a heroic death in action. It is recorded that he was rather disappointed when he read the letter because he had hoped it was his pay warrant. The mistake had happened because during a midnight bayonet charge his company got caught in the wire and machine-gunned. He was hit in the hand and walked two miles to a dressing station and was taken to a base hospital without his name being taken down.

Many of the stories were about the affairs of men at sea. Hull skipper James Elliot of the stern trawler *Sylvia* fell foul of DORA at Milford Haven. He had sailed in, ignorant of the fact that it was a closed port and had ignored a patrol boat warning, the warning lights on Thorn Island which blinded him, three long blasts on a siren and a warning shot. He was fined £5. Back in Hull, Sarah French of 2 Crystal Avenue appeared in the County Court. She was claiming compensation from the Thomas Wilson shipping line for the loss of her husband, forty-five-year-old Walter William who had been washed overboard from the Wilson liner *Guido* on 1 November while the vessel was in transit to Tunis. At that time his average wage was 35s a week and Wilson's had paid her £233 but she wanted £297. Whether she got it was not reported.

In February, the Hull steamer, *Hull Trader*, foundered off South Goodwin lightship with the loss of four hands. An extremely violent south-westerly gale in the channel shifted her cargo and she was swamped by high seas. The survivors were landed at Dover.

Spy phobia continued into 1915. Arthur Harman, a sixteen or seventeen-year-old boy from Hull, was remanded in custody after being tried under DORA. His offence was 'unlawfully attempting to elicit information with respect to the movements, numbers and description of certain of HM Forces with intent to communicate such information to the enemy.' As in the case of the death of William French, an ending was never published.

One snippet showed that not everything was dominated by the war. Two Hull men, Jack Vincent and Lieutenant Cheetham, of the Royal Naval Reserve, were bound for the South Pole with Shackleton. Lieutenant Cheetham was the second officer on the *Endurance* for the journey.

Change seemed to be one of the three constants since the war started. After a meeting of the Yorkshire Agricultural Society, it was decided to abandon the Great Yorkshire Show for the first time since 1837. There would be no further shows until 1920. The 1915 show was scheduled for Hull but was cancelled because of the dislocation of trade and difficulty in obtaining funds from Hull Council.

Another constant was petty crime. William Brown, a twenty-six-year-old dock labourer, was placed on probation for stealing a small quantity of dried apples. Albert Glenton was fined £2 for failing to join his trawler at the appointed time. Mr Israel Cuskins, a home furnisher, pleaded guilty to not providing a dustbin. Judgement was respited (reserved) and he was ordered to pay 20s costs. Robert Stephenson, serving with 4th East Yorkshires, and Freda Last were charged with obtaining 34s under false pretences from the Postmaster General. Stephenson had got her to sign the separation allowance forms in the name of his estranged wife. They admitted their guilt and were remanded for six days.

In late February, the Licensing Committee took a weighty decision, one that upset the managers of Hull's picture halls. They wanted to open on Good Friday for the exhibition of sacred pictures. Permission was refused because it was felt that people should go to church rather than view the pictures, but the committee decided that they would allow concerts!

This blow was followed by an even more serious decision, this time by the government. Lloyd George informed labour leaders they were considering changes to the licensing laws. The government intended to limit the hours of the sale of drink in certain areas to between 12 noon and 2 pm and between 7 and 9 pm. Further restrictions were to follow, restrictions that would be equally unpopular.

Two council departments were struggling with a lack of personnel. A restricted tramcar service was introduced almost overnight when twenty-five Hull tramway men joined up in the space of a few days. The Education Department was similarly short of men. Although this was causing problems, the department was proud of the rate of enlistment, which was higher than in any comparably sized town or city in England. By December 1914, seven office staff, fifty-two Elementary School teachers, four teachers in higher schools and fifteen other education department employees had all enlisted; in fact, one-in-six of all male teachers were in the forces.

Besides the teacher shortage, there were other problems. There was concern over the increasing number of absentees. This was linked to the number of truancy officers who were too busy dealing with the increased number of claims for free meals. It was also discovered that lack of food and sleep were holding many pupils back.

Lighting regulations introduced the previous year were not enforced in the same way across the country. Hull was stricter than many local towns, resulting in the summons of a soldier on leave from Hornsea. He had ridden his motorcycle along Cottingham Road without sufficient light on his bike for his number plate to be seen. People might be summonsed for not showing enough light and prosecuted for showing too much light. Under DORA regulations, houses, shops, offices and public buildings had to prevent internal lighting being visible outside. Contravention of this probably led to more prosecutions than any other regulation. The importance attached was shown by the size of the fines, which increased with each conviction. A fine of £10 was imposed on John Canby for failing to shade the lights in his shop at 63 Market Place. It was a second offence. At the same sitting, the manager of the Black Horse on Carr

Lane was fined five guineas and Robert Grace, a market keeper, was fined £10 for the same offence.

The early months of the war had brought the news of the first dead and wounded. Now came news of the Hull men who had become PoWs. The *Yorkshire Observer* carried a list of 200 Yorkshire men who were prisoners, of which sixty-five were from Hull, including Captain Walter Ford of 78 Cottingham Road; Walter Jordan of 5 Model Dwellings; Hubert Taylor of 122 James Reckitt Avenue; and E.W. Welcome of 191 Boulevard.

Unlike at Christmas, the railway companies suspended all excursions and holiday fares on Good Friday, so a much larger number stayed at home than was usual. Only those who could afford ordinary fares were able to visit the local coastal towns, where, it was suggested, they risked a stray bomb landing in their midst. The two Volunteer Battalions left Hull for South Dalton and a weekend of training. For those left behind, the morning was warm and many visited the parks, but during dinnertime the weather broke. Showers and strong winds sent most home. This did not stop the annual demonstration, which the modern reader would describe as a march or procession, by railwaymen for their orphanage fund, or City playing Arsenal, Hull playing Halifax or Rovers playing Leeds. For a short while on that day, perhaps the war was not at the forefront of everyone's mind.

Eight months into the war, a military funeral was no longer unusual but nevertheless at this stage of the war not common. In early April there was a particularly impressive naval funeral for twenty-nine-year-old naval reservist Amos Drakes, son and sole supporter of his aged mother, Hannah Maria Colley, of 3 York Terrace, Hodgson Street, Hull. He had died at sea on HM Trawler *The Roman* while serving off Scotland. The gunboat HMS *Spanker* was in Victoria Dock and thirty sailors from the boat and the band of the Lancashire Fusiliers gave him a naval funeral. The procession was preceded by a firing party with carbines at 'slope arms' and the band playing the *Dead March from Saul*. The coffin, on a hearse, was covered with the Union Jack and a wreath. A volley was fired over the grave and the ship's carpenter played the *Last Post*.

Writers sometimes proffered to readers advice that seems strange to modern eyes. One interesting piece of advice concerned children and alcohol. 'When children are healthy and vigorous they do not require alcoholic beverages which are best avoided in fear of the formation of an evil habit.' So far so good, but then the advice continued 'but when a child is growing too fast or when its health flags or when the blood is not as healthy as it should be (bad chilblains in winter indicate this) then you often find small regular doses of beer or wine given daily as a medicine for a few weeks of the greatest possible service.' Finally the writer solved the problems of old age when 'the heart becomes weaker and an occasional dose of wine or of the purer spirits, gives that organ a sometimes needed fillip; improving circulation, digestion and the vital functions generally.'

Fund raising continued to occupy many, and Hull gave generously – a French Flag Day in July raised £700. The Master Cutler in Sheffield thanked Hull and district for their donations towards the Razor Fund which had allowed them to send 1,000 razors, strops and brushes to Kitchener's Army. By April the Belgian Relief Fund stood at nearly £500, the Lord Mayor's Fund at just over £500 and the Mother Humber Fund at £780.

Flag Days were a simple method of raising funds. This organisation, headquartered in London, raised money to buy cigarettes.

Apart from occasional shortages, food had been readily available. This, however, was to change, and prices would rise. One of the first foodstuffs to become difficult to afford would be meat. 'A leading Hull butcher forecast much higher meat prices.' This would happen even though there was still sufficient available. The problem was high demand – he reckoned he could sell twice as much – and other areas where there was not enough. 'Buyers from other regions, especially London, were pushing prices up.' The price of sheep in shops had risen 2d a pound recently as a result. Higher prices meant fewer sales, resulting in a nationwide reduction in the number of butchers' shops by 1,000, of which 100 were lost in Hull.

Bacon was another foodstuff that was rising in cost. Cheap imports from America had ruined the British pig industry. However, there was no American bacon available because of the war. Danish bacon was available, but at a price of 80s per cwt it was too expensive for many in Hull.

The Corporation had decided to run Hull Fair even though the ground was needed and though the decision was made not to host the Great Yorkshire Fair, the Spring Fair did take place. Horses were exhibited on the Corporation Field and cattle and sheep in Edwards Place Cattle Market. Attendance was poor as was the show of horses – the better ones had been requisitioned by the army.

Having volunteered for overseas service, the 4th East Yorkshires landed in France on 17 April. Days later the *Hull Daily Mail* published a strong appeal from Lord Nunburnholme, 'The call from the front', appealing to men's patriotism and fear of missing out. It was the usual appeal for volunteers, this time only for the territorials. 'To the young men of Hull who have not yet enlisted. Our local Territorial Troops are now playing their part in the great battle which is raging in Flanders and we are confident that they are doing so with credit to East Yorkshire and to the highest traditions of the British Army. We cannot, alas, expect other than some casualties, to replace which reserve units are now being formed. There is scarcely a family or workshop that is not represented at the front…There is urgent need of you. Come out, and avenge the terrible and inhumane treatment of British prisoners and you will look back with pride in years to come on the step you will, I am confident, take. GOD SAVE THE KING.'

Following Lord Nunburnholme's prophetic words 'expect other than some casualties', came news that the 4th had been involved in an attack in Belgium. Many of the dead and wounded were from Hull. The *Hull Times* reported that the war had been brought suddenly and sharply home to Hull by the losses of the battalion. 'They suffered

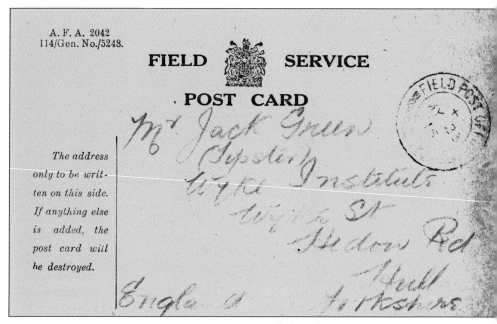

The commonest form of communication from soldiers was the Field Service Post Card. Millions of these were sent.

heavily…advanced as steadily as on parade…Those who were killed died a glorious death on the field of honour…Colonel Shaw was shot at the head of the attack.'

What the public did not know was the full extent of the casualties. The paper informed them that the losses included Colonel Shaw, Major Theilman, Captain Farrell plus five men from Beverley, five from Bridlington, one from Driffield and twelve from Hull, one of whom was C.W. Grindell, son of Councillor Grindell. The battalion war diary reported the officer casualties, twelve other ranks killed, sixty-six wounded, sixteen wounded and missing and a further seven missing. It was appropriate that, in the same issue, Red Cross Flags were being sold to raise funds for another motor ambulance to help the wounded.

How well had Hull and district done in raising recruits? On 28 April, Major Saunders of the 15th Recruiting Area published the following table.

Summary of recruits raised in the 15th recruiting district					
Type of unit	Place of enlistment	Number enlisted	Totals	Enlistment period to:	Other information
Regular and New Armies	Outside Hull	1,002		26 Apr 1915	Popul. of Hull & East Riding – 444,780
	Pryme Street	2,936		26 Apr 1915	
	City Hall	6,855		26 Apr1915	
	East Hull	215		30 Sep 1914	Office closed
	West Hull	1,917		31 Jan 1915	Office closed
	Walton Street	1,007		19 Sep 1914	Office closed [Frontiersmen & C.
	Specials area	140		Approximately	Motor drivers, Flying Corps, Sports Batt.
	Waggoners Reserve	1,010			Were registered prior to the war service outside East Riding
	National	115	15,287	26 Apr 1915	
Territorial Force	East Riding units	3,726		31 Mar 1915	
	North Riding units	572		31 Mar 1915	Located in East Riding
	Officers	90	4,388	Approximately	
Royal Navy	Regulation Navy	176		31 Mar 1915	
	Re-engagements	161		23 Apr 1915	Ex-Royal Navy
	Reserve for war	2,375		23 Apr 1915	Minesweepers & C.
	Specials	195		23 Apr 1915	Patrol ships & C.
	Officers	50		Approximately	
	Coast Watchers	40	2,997		From Hull only
			22,672		
Volunteer Training Corps	East Riding		2,400		
Firms producing munitions of war			No record		

Prior to this table being published, there had been yet another recruitment drive. On 13 March there had been 'a great "Recruiting March" through Hull, in which some 10,000 troops were concerned.'

Once again alcohol raised its head. Lloyd George raised the duty, resulting in prices in Hull rising. Spirits rose by 2s 6d a bottle and 1d a glass. The cost of wine increased by up to 2s a bottle and bottled beer 2s a dozen pint bottles. Fortunately for drinkers, the tax was repealed.

Alcohol often featured in cases at the Magistrates Court. Robert Jenkins was sent to prison for thirty days for making a false attestation when presenting himself for enlistment. When he had enlisted in 11th East Yorkshires he had said he had no previous military service. He was arrested when it was discovered he had served in the East Yorkshires. He claimed his false statement was because he was drunk at the time. An exciting chase and assault were the result of drinking too much in June. George Moore, an elderly man of foreign appearance, was charged with assaulting Ada Scarron, Lilian Ellis and Mary Snee. Already intoxicated, he went into a pub and during a conversation with some women mentioned some plans. This excited several fishermen who took him for a German spy and chased him. He ran down Caroline Place, into a relative's home at 1 Victoria Place, where he assaulted Scarron and her mother. He was ejected and seen opening a knife while running along the terrace. With the knife he struck Snee over the eye as she attempted to protect Scarron, and he also cut the thumb of a girl, Lillian Ellis. He denied the offence and said he might have struck them in self-defence. He was fined 21s or fifteen days.

A second great uncle the writer never got to meet. Pte George William Hedley Cook of the 2nd/4th East Yorkshire Regiment in early 1915. In 1917 he was transferred to the Durham Light Infantry. He is listed on the Tyne Cot Memorial.

Walter posing for a photograph before he left for the front. He was serving with the Royal Engineers (East Riding), 529 Field Company which went to Western Front in September 1915.

For the War.

1914—League 🔵 of Honour.

For Women and Girls of the Empire.

Motto: "Strength and Honour."

Member's Promise: "I promise, by the help of God, to do all that is in my power to uphold the honour of our Empire and its defenders in this time of war, by Prayer, Purity, and Temperance."

Member's Signature ....

Enrolling Officer *L. Foster.* ....

Temperance War Pledge: "I promise, by the help of God, to abstain from all Alcoholic Drinks, as beverages, during the war, and to encourage others to do the same."

Member's Signature ....

Enrolling Officer ....

An unissued membership card for the 1914 League of Honour. Members promised to uphold the honour of the Empire and abstain from alcohol for the duration.

It was not just civilians who got drunk. Thomas Handley appeared in the dock charged with being drunk and incapable, wearing his volunteer uniform – no doubt to impress the bench and hopefully get off more lightly. He had been found lying across the footpath in a drunken condition. After expressing his regret and telling them he was a volunteer, he was fined 7s 6d.

Some news seemed remote, like the sinking of the *Lusitania*, until the local aspect was revealed. It also shows that with deadlines looming, facts were not always checked. An on-board steward, J.J. Bostock had a brother and sister in Scarborough – interestingly, he is not listed as a crew member in modern research – and Mrs Nore Clarke, sister-in-law of Mr Neville Clarke of Bridlington, who was coming from Toronto on holiday, was one who died.

Hull's nautical connection continued throughout the war. In May, Mr G. Lacey, a coal exporter, donated a cheque for £200. This was to be handed over to the master and crew of the first vessel belonging to a Humber or Ouse port who satisfied the Mayor that they had, after 19 May, sunk a German submarine.

As inhabitants of a fishing port, men went out to sea knowing well that they could be sunk or captured by the enemy. The trawler *Argyll* had been torpedoed without warning on 15 May leaving three survivors. Most were in their bunks at the time of the explosion. Among those killed was the engineer, Jack Cowlam, whose wife would lose her father on 27 May when the *Southward Ho!* went missing. Another incident, this time an explosion, clearly shows how closely-related many of the trawler families were. In November an explosion claimed the lives of three men, all of whom were related: James Hodgson, of 4 Herbert's Terrace, husband of Harriet, left a widow and three children; Harriet's brother, James Hepworth, of 1 Ivy Villas, was the chief engineer; and Charles Bailey, aged eighteen, was the son of Mrs Hepworth, by her first marriage. The rest of the crew were saved.

On 18 May, the trawlers *Duke of Wellington* and *Euclid* were captured by a torpedo boat while fishing on the Dogger Bank. The *Hull Daily Mail* reported what had happened. 'When the Grimsby trawler *Cetus*, owned by the Grimsby and North Sea Steam Trawling Company, Ltd, arrived at Grimsby last night, Skipper S Wright, of Bridge Street, reported a curious incident. Whilst fishing in the North Sea on Tuesday, 110 miles from Spurn, he observed a derelict boat, and upon going up to it found it was marked "EUCLID - HULL." In the boat were suits of clothes, lifebelts (also marked "Euclid, Hull"), a keg of water, some provisions, and a basket of fish. The rope warp, together with a bass fender, had been slashed by some sharp instrument. The boat was undoubtedly one belonging to a fishing vessel, and in the opinion of Skipper Wright was of the type used for boarding a fish cutter. It was too large to get on board the *Cetus* without considerable difficulty…(so) he took possession of the clothing, etc, and then left the boat to drift away. Skipper Wright states that the indications pointed to the boat's occupants having had to leave the craft in a hurry.'

The skipper of the *Cetus* gave his opinion of what had happened. 'The *Euclid* had been attacked by a German Submarine, and the fishermen had been ordered to their boat. They had put into the boat all their effects; he had found a leather pocket-book and a Union card belonging to one of the engineers, and 1s 10d in money. He surmised that something then happened which had prevented them getting into their boat, and that the submarine had evidently been compelled to go away in a hurry and had taken the crew prisoners. The whole thing, of course is a complete mystery, but that the boat had been set adrift from the trawler is shown by the fact that, when examined, the boat's painter was found to have been slashed across, evidently by a sword.'

The men on board were taken prisoner and sent to Stadtvogtei, a pre-war civilian prison in Berlin. They wrote to ask for help from the fishermen of Hull. 'We have neither tobacco, cigarettes, nor anything else, as we lost everything when we were sunk by a torpedo boat. We are the only two crews interned in Germany from Hull…we all think there will be plenty of our pals who would like to help us in Hull, and as we have to buy our own soap to wash our clothes, and anything extra we want, being without the means of buying the same, and thinking any small contribution would help us to tidy over our difficulty. Reading, clothes, and cigarette papers would also be thankfully received as it costs nothing for postage for a parcel or a letter.'

Two days after the loss of the *Euclid* and *Duke of Wellington*, the trawler *Sebastian* was lost. The next day the trawler *Sabrina* struck a mine. Among those who died was Deck Hand Arthur Johnson of 343 Hawthorne Avenue. He was just fifteen-years old.

THREE LOST IN ONE HULL FAMILY

Three members of the Hodgson family were killed by an explosion on a trawler.

'From the beginning of the war British propaganda had stirred up dark emotions in the British public with stories of the atrocities perpetrated on the French and Belgians by the Germans for the least little provocation.' During the year there had been a story about a crucified British soldier discounted after the war for lack of proof but in fact proved in 2002 to have actually occurred, though the soldier was Canadian, not British. The sinking of the *Lusitania* on 7 May by a German submarine, with the loss of over 1,000 lives, further fuelled anti-German feeling far more than these stories or the more local sinkings. Rioting crowds, mostly spontaneous but some planned, attacked German shops, smashing windows and looting. In Hull, as in London, the crowds rioted. As Florence Mower recalled: 'There was a pork butcher's down Wincolmlee, Barmston Street... There was the shop downstairs and they had a piano upstairs. They broke all the windows and I can remember seeing the piano actually thrown through the upstairs window. Where the poor butcher and his wife and children were, I really don't know. They just raided them all. It was terrible.'

One Hull pork butcher was in luck. One of those about to go on a planned rampage warned him about the coming attacks. On 12 May, Charles Hohenrein received an anonymous letter:

'Dear Sir,
I belong to a secret gang but I want to be your friend. I wish to warn you that your shop's in danger and perhaps *life* for God's sake take this as a warning from one who wishes you no harm (Don't treat this as an Idel [sic] joke) –
Friendship
I have signed friendship but I don't know you and you don't know me.'

Also enclosed were the details

BEVERLEY OFFICER KILLED IN THE DARDANELLES.

LIEUT. G. WOOLL.

Amongst the official list of casualties in the Dardanelles, published on Tuesday of this week, the death of a Beverley soldier, who had a distinguished military career, is announced. This is Lieutenant and Quartermaster G. Wooll, of the Northumberland Fusiliers, who had risen from the ranks. Lieut. Wooll, who was in his 41st year, was a native of Lockington, but was very well known and locally respected in Beverley, where his widowed mother has resided for many years.

At the age of 17 he enlisted into the 1st Battalion Northumberland Fusiliers, and retired after 21 years' service, holding two years ago. For the last 14 years he held the rank of sergeant major, and a greater portion of his services with the colours was fulfilled in India. His active service record was one to be proud of. He possessed the following decorations: Medal for the Nile Expedition and Egyptian medal, 1898; the Queen's medal with two clasps for the South African Campaign, 1899-1902; medal for the Mohmand Expedition, 1908, the Delhi Durbar medal, and a long service and good conduct medal. During the South African Campaign he was recommended for a commission, but did not accept the offer.

On his returning from the Army in December, 1913, Lieutenant Wooll took up his residence at Ealing, London, where he was the proprietor of a confectioners' business. On August 19th of last year he rejoined the Northumberland Fusiliers, and on the 24th November last was appointed lieutenant of the 4th Service Battalion of that regiment. He left England for the Dardanelles on June 13th, and strange to relate he was killed on August 20th, exactly one year to the day after rejoining the Army.

Another sad coincidence is the fact that when the news reached the widow at Ealing on Tuesday of last week, their only daughter was celebrating her birthday by entertaining a few school friends to tea. Deceased's aged mother was also visiting her daughter-in-law at the time.

Pte. W. SLANEY.   Pte. R. S. KNOWLES.

Private W. Slaney and Private R. S. Knowles, two Hull chums, 6th East Yorks, now at the Dardanelles.

LOST FROM THE TRAWLER JASPER

J. L. DAVISON.   J. MULHOLLAND

J. L. Davison, husband of Mrs Davison, Subway-street, and son of Mr and Mrs Davison, 289, Hessle-road, Hull.
John Mulholland, whose home was with his aunt, Mrs Edith Mower, 16, Subway-street, Hull. Both were amongst the men lost from the trawler Jasper.

R. H. LANGLEY.   Rifleman W. RUDD.

Pte. P. CULLINEY.   Pte. J. PRITCHARD

Pte. J. GRIFFIN.   E. GARDNER.

Richard H. Langley, mine-sweeper, who was drowned off the mine-sweeper No. 83, near the Dardanelles, on August 21st. He was a brother-in-law of Sergeant Foster, who was killed at the Dardanelles on May 25th.
Rifleman W. Rudd, 9th Rifle Brigade, whose home is at 85, Barmston-street. He has been wounded, and is now in hospital in France.
Private Patsy Culliney, who has been in the firing line since January, having been wounded in the battle of Hooge on August 9th. Before enlistment he resided with his parents at 97 Eton-street, Hessle-road.
Private J. Pritchard, 1st E. Yorks, in writing home to his wife at 7, Symons-terrace, Beane street, states that he is wounded in the hip and arm and is now in hospital at Le Treport.
Private Jos. Griffin, 1st E. Yorks, wounded and now in the Lord Derby War Hospital, Warrington.
Ernest Gardner, 86, Ryde-street, first class stoker, H.M.S. Diadem; joined June, 1915.

Typical obituaries from the Hull Times.

Funeral procession for the men killed when the Germans shelled the submarine E14 *in Danish waters. They were in transit to Paragon for burial in other parts of the country. On arrival in Hull one was sent across to Goole.*

the butcher needed about the dates of the planned attacks.

On the same day an unstamped letter arrived, costing the butcher two pence in surcharge costs. The letter explained the reason for his concern:

'Dear Sir,
I hope you got my last letter and I hope you have taken notice of it as your shop is going to be broken up on —- and —- . I dare not let you know too much as I would be found and I would have to suffer. The reason I have taken such an interest in warning you is because when I was a boy your parents and those who kept your shop were very good to me many a time when I was hungry and needed bread so you see I wish you no harm in any way. Your shop is not the only shop but there are others and I am warning you and I shall have to carry out my work when I am ordered by my chief the captain. Sir, if you will put a letter in the *Daily Mail* I will know you have got my letter. I do not mean a bold one but one of a mild kind. The reason is to av_____

LUSITANIA
Friendship __2ⁿᵈ'

Anti-German feeling ran high during 1915, resulting in many companies with German sounding names closing.

Throughout Hull there was an orgy of violence. The local press reported the attack on Charles Hohenrein's shop. 'About midnight a crowd of youths and men were in Waterworks Street, assuming a threatening attitude in front of the premises of Mr. Hohenrein, pork butcher. Later two youths threw a large stone through the window, smashing the same. The delinquents were pointed out to the police and arrested, the crowd making no attempt at rescue. A Territorial remonstrated with the offenders.' The irony was that the butcher's son was interned in Germany as an enemy alien.

In 1914 women had been relegated to sewing, knitting and other activities that they could do from home or locally. However, times were changing, and in May the *Hull Times* wrote about women who felt that there was more that they could do: Miss Pritchard, Superintendent of the Jubilee Nurses Home, had gone to Serbia; the vicar of Dairycoates' daughter, Miss Butler, had left Hull to nurse further afield; and Lady Laurence had started a scheme for canteens for munitions workers. It was noted that many others had already left to work abroad and in other parts of the country.

Usually charities asked for money or people's time. In June, Brigadier General Dixon asked for sandbags, assuring 'the good people of Hull, that providing thousands of sandbags [was] a great kindness in so much that they are the means of saving valuable, and to some, inexpressibly dear lives.' He hoped that subscribers would be forthcoming to provide the sandbags. Shortly after this request, the 2nd/4th East Yorkshires appealed to the public for cricket sets, footballs and prizes.

The boarded windows of Schumm's Pork Butchers, damaged in the 1915 rioting.

Summer brought the war to the city and a return to mob violence against Germans or those thought to be German. The first Zeppelin raid occurred on 6 June. The attack by *L9* only happened because the wind prevented Kapitänleutnant Mathy from reaching London. After following the railway lines from Bridlington to Hull, he dropped flares to light up the docks. There were no defences other than the guns of HMS *Adventure* which was being repaired in Earl's Yard, noted by the Germans as a light battery without searchlights.

Thirteen high-explosive bombs and fifty incendiaries, dropped on the Old Town and Drypool area, resulted in the destruction of forty houses and shops, killing a total of twenty-four people and injuring a further forty, including children. Total damage was estimated at £44,795. The Brasso building at Reckitt's Kingston Works was hit but the cost of repair was a mere £18 10s. However, as a result of this the company took out the air raid insurance it had turned down a few months earlier.

Mobs retaliated on the ground by sacking shops, such as Kress and Wagner and 'The Pork Butcher' Hohenrein's, believed to belong to Germans. As a result of incidents, Hohenrein appealed to the Chief Constable's office to confirm his British nationality.

The response confirmed Hohenrein's identity. 'The bearer, Mr C. H. Hohenrein, is a British-born subject whom I have known since his youth. He is a man of the highest integrity and honour, and I have the most implicit confidence and reliance in him. He is well known to most of the leading citizens in this district.'

This together with the fact that his son was in British Army, his brother George and nephew William had been interned in Germany, the offer of £500 to charity if anyone could prove he was not British, and that he was never interned, did not stop the threats and insults. Like others, he closed the business down, until, after changing his name to Ross, he successfully re-opened in November.

Nearly eighty years later, an elderly woman recalled her experience of that first raid. 'It was dark, but there was a funny flickering light in the bedroom when father came and woke us up. He was very quiet and calm and told us all to get dressed and go downstairs as quick as we could.'

Without net curtains to block her view, she saw that the coal house next to her bedroom was on fire. It was the result of an incendiary bomb. 'People – strangers – started coming into the house and taking furniture out and putting wet sheets up at the walls to stop the fire spreading.' They were bundled out and across the road to a neighbours, where, as the bombs were still falling, they were put in a cupboard under the stairs. 'It was wick with blackclocks [alive with black beetles] but we stayed there until all was quiet – they were not as bad as the bombs...The smell of burning was everywhere.' Unfortunately not everyone who had helped had assisted out of altruism. One person had an ulterior motive. 'Worst of all, somebody had pinched the mantelpiece clock that had next week's rent in it.'

Buzzer nights, air raid or not, were eagerly awaited by many children. Dependent on the time the 'release system' sounded (the all clear), a disturbed night might mean a later school start of 9.45 am or even a half day off. Every cloud has a silver lining.

The Mother Humber Fund raised money to help local old and poor with food vouchers and coal. This group of dancers from Madam S. Harrah's dance school performed at the Tivoli to raise funds for 'Mother Humber'.

After the first raid, the government responded with the best available defence it had; nothing. In early July, the military installed a gun at The Forge, a flat-roofed, reinforced concrete building at what would become Rose, Downs and Thompson. The problem was, and this information was classified, that the gun was not real. Even the managing director, Mr Charles Downs, thought it was real but the workforce, who had seen it put in place surreptitiously during the lunch break, knew better. The gunners manned it from 8 pm until 5 am, ready to fire at the given signal. During the day it was guarded, cleaned and covered over.

It was removed and disposed of after Mr Downs expressed concern about what would happen when the local population, who had great confidence in it, learned the truth. Questions were even raised in the House of Commons. Someone submitted a mock tender to 'conform to the requirements of "The New Wooden Gun Department of the War Office.".'

Initially 'some left home to sit out raids in East Park. After a couple of experiences, most decided it was safer to be at home than risk the danger to health from being out at night.' Those with a billiard table

The ruins of Edwin Davis' shop on Market Place. Smoke is partially obscuring Holy Trinity church.

found a previously unguessed-of use for it – hiding under it during raids. After a raid, although they knew it was not allowed, children went around looking for pieces of shrapnel as souvenirs.

The first raid was followed by the looting of houses and shops owned by Germans. Guarding these premises were men of 17th Battalion Northumberland Fusiliers who were back in Hull prior to moving to Catterick Bridge. They found it a very uncongenial job but it had a bright side. 'The people living in the street were very good' and brought them tea throughout the night.

A postcard produced after the June raid.

Some residents were more concerned about the raid and the alarms than others. Nervousness caused by the alarms and threat of attack caused Elizabeth Richardson to attempt suicide. She had thrown herself into Sutton Drain. She was discharged on the understanding that her husband looked after her in the future.

In the first few days of the war, it was suggested that women might become tram conductors. The hiring of women conductors led to a tramways dispute in which the Corporation acceded in all points except their retention of the right to hire conductors. The Mayor wanted the women given a fair chance and felt that people should realise they were

The entrance to West Park, originally known as Western District Park. It was constructed on land bought at £1,400 per acre from the North Eastern Railway Company in 1878. It was to spaces such as this that people went on potential raid nights.

living in changed times. The employment of women was an experiment to meet abnormal conditions.

There was yet another change, and an important one for British citizens; the identity card. On 15 July, the National Registration Act 1915 was passed. This act required all men and women, between the ages of fifteen and sixty-five years of age, to register at their home on 15 August 1915. Some 29 million forms were issued across England, Scotland and Wales. The returned forms were collected shortly after 15 August 1915 and compiled by the local authority. A summary of the register was passed to the Registrar General, who compiled statistics, but the actual forms were retained at a local level. In Hull the forms were given out by volunteers on 9 August.

That night Hull was lucky. After waiting for darkness off the East Coast, airship *L9* came in over land and more or less headed for Hull. Fortunately the blackout and ground mist made it difficult to orientate the airship and, after circuiting twice while repairs were made to the rudder, it had drifted. What the crew thought was Hull was actually Goole. After the raid, they claimed to have caused severe damage to Hull docks. In fact they had destroyed ten dwellings, damaged some warehouses and killed sixteen people in Goole twenty miles west.

An unpopular change was the new postal rates. After prices holding steady for nearly twenty years, the weight of a 1d postage letter dropped to 1oz from 4oz, a 2oz letter cost 2d and each additional 2oz was ½d. Other charges also went up. Everything was starting to become more expensive.

At the start of the war, Lord Curzon had spoken in the City Hall, addressing the reasons for the war and for enlistment. Many members of the Labour Party had been against Britain's involvement and had openly questioned Britain's role. Some believed it was right for Britain to be involved. One of those was Ben Tillett, a Trade Union leader and

In August people received this form. It provided the government with accurate manpower statistics and a record of those whose employment was essential for the nation and those who could eventually be conscripted.

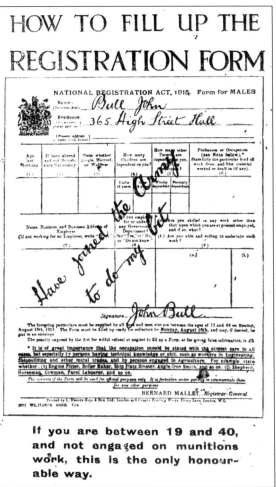

After completing the form, each person aged between 15 and 65 received a card like this that had to be carried at all times and shown when asked.

NATIONAL

REGISTRATION

ACT, 1915.

future politician. Like Lord Curzon he gave a rousing address at the City Hall. This address was to help boost munitions output at a time of munitions shortages.

Another shortage was found in the number of men who wanted to join the army. To attract volunteers and commemorate the first anniversary of the war, the 3rd/4th East Yorkshires held a recruiting march. How much enthusiasm had waned is shown by their needing to attract 800 men, 400 for themselves and 400 for the 2nd/4th in Newcastle. The battalion marched through the town and held open-air meetings at which the Secretary of the East Riding TF Association asked for every able-bodied man to come forward in defence of his hearth and home and the women and children dependent upon him.

This message was reinforced by a schoolgirl's letter and a cry to avenge Edith Cavell. The unnamed girl asked: 'Why should not the big, healthy men who stand behind public bars serving married men with pints of beer, who should be at home with their wives and children, enlist?...The recruiting sergeants take married men from their homes where they have wives and children. I think the unmarried men should enlist before making the married men enlist... Some of the women who are not married, who stand behind toyshop counters and other places as well: why shouldn't they help their King and country? – I am.'

The death of Edith Cavell was used to make men feel guilty. 'Men of Britain, will you stand aside and allow such things as the execution of Miss Cavell? It might have been your wife, your mother, your sweetheart, or your child! Come forward at once, and help to crush those whose only motto is "Might is Right".'

These were followed by the Anti-German Union opening up a campaign shop in Prospect Street and holding public meetings at which Lord Headley and Sir George Makgill spoke. The union was pro-British, anti-socialist and wanted every aspect of German life and culture removed, especially in business. It is thought to have had around 10,000 members by the end of the war.

Feelings were further inflamed by editorials like that of the *Eastern Morning News*. 'The time has come when we must treat all Germans as our daily foes. Too long we have been parleying with the enemy within the gate. We must begin our warfare at home. We have too much of the German in England since the war began. We have husbanded

Route marches through the city were used to encourage enlistment. Here the 17th Northumberland Fusiliers parade through the town during the 1915 'great route march'.

A street lined with people watching the 'great route march'. How useful it was is unclear.

spies. We have given liberty – not to say licence – to all sorts of conditions of Germans. There must be no more of it. We must look upon the Germans as people not to be trusted.'

In reply to a written request, the Prime Minister provided details of losses to October.

	Western Front		Other fronts	
	Officers	Other ranks	Officers	Other ranks
Killed in action	4,401	63,059	6,660	94,992
Wounded	9,169	225,716	12,633	304,882
Missing	1,567	61,134	2,000	72,177

Perhaps the publication of casualty figures had an effect on recruitment as well as the above, or perhaps it was the Derby scheme that was ending in December, and the dislike of the threat of conscription? Recruitment increased. Some men were still keen to enlist but only with permission. During October, eleven staff of the Sculcoates workhouse sent a petition to the chairman and Guardians of the Sculcoates Union asking permission to enlist. 'We the undersigned members of your staff, respectfully beg to ask your permission to offer our services to the country. We feel very keenly the serious situation…and the urgent appeal for men…Many of us have had such a step in view for months…have had in mind the necessities and the welfare of our dependents…we desire to obtain your assurance that in the event of our offer being accepted our position would be open to us should we return at the conclusion of the war.'

They did not want only that their jobs would be retained, but also that their army pay would be made up to their civilian wage by the board. Eleven wanted to join the army and one to do munitions work – he did not want his wage made up because he would earn more in munitions. Eight were married and four single. Their request was agreed to be unopposed.

At the end of November, recruitment in Hull was brisk. However, it was hampered by new regulations and the Derby scheme. There was also concern over the issue of armlets to signify men who had enlisted and gone on the reserve. Most volunteered under the Derby scheme, which would take married men last and only when needed. In response to this, the whole of the male staff of the Corporation Telephone Section enlisted at City Hall, followed by the office staff of the Wilson Line.

The rush to voluntarily enlist is shown by a short article in the *Hull Times*: a man confined to the house with influenza was attested; one evening as the City Hall was closing men were 'clambering at the side doors' to get in; the supply of armlets ran out; the entire staff of Hull Dairies enlisted en masse.

How many enlisted is not recorded. The figures for men needed in the East Yorkshire Regiment shows how severe the shortage of men was becoming. Both regular battalions were at strength, but the 3rd needed 800 men; the 4th also needed 800; the 5th, 900; the 9th, 1,700; and the 14th required 2,000.

The effect the war was having on Hull's trade is clearly shown by coal exports. For the week ending 26 October, 33,515 tons were shipped to Holland, Sweden, Denmark and Guernsey. Comparable dates for 1914 and 1913 were 43,201 and 83,068 tons respectively.

However, life was not all gloom. People still got married and enjoyed their celebrations. Probably the biggest of the year occurred just before Christmas. Over 100 members of staff of Earle's Shipyard were entertained to dinner at the Grosvenor Hotel. The occasion was the marriage of Lieutenant Earle to George Daphne Fitzgeorge, granddaughter of the Duke of Cambridge.

Innovation was key to charitable donations. The egg fund wanted people to buy a 1d stamp so eggs, which were scarce so late in the year, could be bought for wounded soldiers. In less than a year it had sent thirteen million eggs to wounded troops abroad or in the UK. A national auction was another way to raise money. In 1916 local beekeepers gave honey to *The Times,* which auctioned it off across the country.

A slow but sure way to raise funds was an auction. In December, £800 was realised in a sale run by Wells and Sons. Sixty lots of coal realised from 25s to 35s a ton; a 75mm French artillery shell case sold for £11 10s; 12½lb of Stilton went for £4 4s; a French bomb sold for £4 10s. There were even articles sent from abroad. Private Inesty, serving in the Dardanelles, sent two silver mounted pipes in a case which could be bought for between 5s and 6s normally but here they reached 35s. The money raised went to a range of war charities. Perhaps some went to the Children's Christmas Fund for poor Hull children that was asking for donations and gifts.

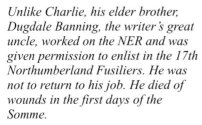

Unlike Charlie, his elder brother, Dugdale Banning, the writer's great uncle, worked on the NER and was given permission to enlist in the 17th Northumberland Fusiliers. He was not to return to his job. He died of wounds in the first days of the Somme.

If you can't fight, wear a big hat. The young man wearing his service cap is the writer's paternal grandfather. Of this group of four friends who enlisted together a few days after the war started, two were killed at Gallipoli, one was wounded and the other captured by the Turks. He died after the war because of the treatment he had received in captivity. Although Private Bilton was a railwayman, he was released by the Hull and Barnsley Railway with a job promise for his return.

The year finished with lighting-up restrictions, casualty lists and the finale of a murder. In September 1915, Mrs Hilda Bertha MacDonald (née Charlotte Kent), twenty-nine-years-old, was murdered at the home of Mrs Eliza Rodgers, Brass Castle Hill, in Pocklington. It was a crime of passion and jealousy. John William McCartney appeared in Hull in 1913 posing as a single man. He met Charlotte Kent and they lived together off Campbell Street, Hull, until he enlisted in June 1915 under the alias of Harry MacDonald. When

ergeant Fryer was regarded as the best recruiter in
orkshire after he won the £10 prize from Lord
unburnholme. He recruited 437 men for the army.

*An advert for
the Christmas
pantomime.*

*Not all who wanted to go received
permission from their employer. Charlie
Banning, the writer's great uncle, was an
express train driver for the NER who had
to continue driving throughout the war.*

*Even with the first and second
line regiments filled there was
still the need for more men.
Initially they were replacements
for the first line and to guard
strategic areas around the
country. Later they would be
used to fill the ranks of any unit
that needed them.*

A 1915 fancy dress Christmas party showing costumes across the ages and countries.

A Red Cross ambulance paid for by public subscription.

A Christmas 1915 certificate given to children who provided gifts or donations to help those serving their King and Country.

he moved to Ousethorpe Camp she followed and took lodgings in Pocklington. They married in July but quickly he showed his true self. This culminated in his cutting his wife's throat and then his own. He pleaded not guilty at his trial in York but was found guilty of murder and sentenced to death. His execution, set for 15 December, was deferred when he appealed against the sentence. His counsel submitted that the jury had been misdirected and that he was insane, like his mother's brother and his father's brother. The application was refused and he was executed in Wakefield gaol on 29 December.

How did the *Hull Daily Mail* leader writer feel about the year? 'It is a sad and tragic year of which we take pensive farewell today. As we look back upon it we wonder at the capacity of human nature for endurance. We begin to understand the terrific storms through which our fathers' generations passed, we realise the unity of the English race. Never before in the history of the world has there been such a loss of life. Blood has indeed flowed like water...The record of the year seems almost too horrible to look back at, the more particularly as there is no halt...Our courage and determination remain unshaken and we shall enter 1916 with undismayed eyes and unshaken hope of victory.'

How would Hull celebrate the New Year?

The second war Christmas and The Hull Times *once again wished its readers near and far a Happy Christmas.*

CHAPTER 3

1916:
The Realisation

'The old year passed out in Hull quietly. The Humber ferry ran with difficulty because of the strong winds. Buzzers and sirens were forbidden under DORA. No church bells rung. Pubs closed at 9 pm. The main topic of conversation was the loss of HMS *Natal*, sunk by an internal explosion in the Cromarty Firth on 30 December 1915. Places of amusement were filled and there were numerous private parties. As midnight approached boys and girls filled the streets.' Fortunately the ensuing casualty list on the next day was small.

Calls for moderation in consumption in Hull, as across the country, had fallen on many deaf ears. The object was to reduce imports but Board of Trade figures revealed the opposite. Total food, drink and tobacco imported during 1915 cost £381,900,901, an increase of £84,931,694. The largest contributor to the total was grain and flour, up £32,726,422 over 1914.

Crime continued – 1916 would be no different to 1915. Early cases involved a nursemaid stealing a wedding ring, a diamond ring and a pearl brooch from a house in Pearson Park, a drunk Norwegian sailor attempting to commit suicide, and child neglect, of which there had been a number of cases in 1915.

Charities raised awareness by letting the public know how much they had contributed and how it was being used. The Tobacco Fund for the 4th East Yorkshires stood at a whopping £300 but this was for smokes, not the socks they were appealing for, while the Belgian Relief Fund had £380.

The Mother Humber Fund was used to supplement OAPs; to help widows left with young families; to assist in cases of sickness; to extend aid to people overwhelmed by sudden misfortunes; and to provide fire guards in poor homes. Since it had re-opened in November 1915, it had issued forty-two one-shilling, and fifty-three two-shilling, grocery orders and given out ninety-nine coal orders.

Both Hull newspapers had their own fund for which they constantly asked for gifts and subscriptions. How had they helped the fighting man? They had sent out 720 tins of acid drops; over 2,000 razors; 1,410 cardigan jackets and sweaters; 1,550 pencils; 50,000 cigarettes; 460 lbs of tobacco; 240 tins of mints; 250 lbs of chocolate; 200 plum puddings; as well as gramophones, records, boxing gloves, table games, footballs and more.

A sure sign that the war was having a heavy impact on civilian life came towards the end of January: at a Yorkshire Cricket Club meeting, Hull, Leeds Police, Rotherham, Sheffield, Whitworth Colliery and York announced they were no longer able to play matches in the league. Another sign was that the *Hull Times* as well as other papers reduced their page count. This was due to government control of paper supplies and a general shortage. People were told to order their copies as fewer were to be printed. Worse still, beer and stout prices went up by ½d from 17 April!

The December rush to enlist as a Derby man produced a large number of potential recruits. By the end of the first week in January, the total was 18,000. One interesting fact the process revealed was that

TWO HULL BROTHERS.

Lance-Corpl. A. WENHAM. **Pte. W. WENHAM, R.A.M.C.**

The photos are of two Hull brothers, who are in His Majesty's Forces. Their home is 88, Victor-street, Holderness-road, Hull. In a letter home Lance-Corporal A. Wenham, of the 1st Coldstream Guards, says:—"I was sorry about the parcel. I don't suppose I shall ever get it now, but never mind; perhaps some of the poor beggars in the trenches have got it, and I am sure they can do with it. It is terrible in those trenches. I had a week of it before I got wounded; raining all the time, and never stopped. We were up past our knees in water all the time, so you can have a guess what it was like, and that crowned it when they started shelling us. It began to get a bit hot when the big 'Jack Johnson' started buzzing over, but we got quite used to them. But it was not very nice when you saw a pal on your right or left getting knocked down and killed. I lost my best pal the very first time we were in action. He was next to me when we were in action. He was next to me when he got killed. He got struck right in the head with a bullet, but it couldn't be helped. It had to be. I was very lucky the same shell didn't catch me. We did not half see some awful sights when we were there. There was a draught went up the other day for our battalion, so I expect there won't be another sent up for a week or two yet, but I don't know, so if you are going to send anything send it as soon as you can."

The Wenham brothers. As long as no places were mentioned, the letters printed from soldiers could be quite detailed about the horrors of war.

THANK GOD
I CAN SEE THE
CHURCH ARMY
HUT

A regular Flag Day was that for the Church Army Hut Fund. Money raised was used to provide accommodation for travelling soldiers.

some of the married men were only eighteen. Over the last seven days of the Derby scheme, 6-12 December, the enlistment figures were: 418, 410, 885, 2,322, 4,319, 4,378 and, on the final day, Sunday, 1,660.

Under the Derby scheme, men were put in age groups to be called on a strict rota. Technically it had closed, but on 10 January was re-opened. Shortly afterwards the Lord Mayor appealed to the young men of Hull to come forward whilst voluntary enlistment under the group system was still open. 'Hull has done so well in the past that I am anxious its reputation should not be spoiled by it being found out later on that a large number of young men have had to be fetched under a compulsory system...Over 30,000 men have gone from Hull. WON'T YOU JOIN THEM?'

Shortly after this appeal, readers were warned that the Military Service Act was in operation from February 1916. After that there would be no voluntary enlistment, just conscription.

In March the army started to call up men from classes two to twelve, all men aged 19-30, which corresponded to the Derby men born 1886 to 1896 who had already been called. Married men began to be called up in late April with the youngest first, and by July men aged 41 were being called.

All enlistments under the group system ceased at the end of April. Any married man not registered could now be called for immediate service. At the same time, married groups up to 51 were told they were to report at the end of May for enlistment. This gave them a month to put their affairs in order.

Men called up with their class were conscripts and had a right to appeal to a tribunal. Hull's tribunal was set up in March with sixteen members from Hull and the East Riding, including Lord Deramore and other prominent citizens. Their function was to adjudicate upon claims for exemption upon the grounds of performing civilian work of national importance, domestic hardship, health and conscientious objection.

Conscientious Objectors received a mixed reception, particularly those who had suddenly become very religious or adopted very left-wing views. Most were reviled as just being cowards, but one letter writer in Hull, who called himself 'A Freeman', felt otherwise. 'I am sorry to find, sir, that the conscientious objector is not given this credit of his convictions. The people seem to jeer at him. But if a man's conscience tells him that he ought to fight so he ought; if it tells him he ought not to fight, he ought not. Everyman is born into the world a free agent, and should be allowed to please himself. It is the man who is not afraid to stand alone who can stand the best in a crowd.'

Often those with legitimate reasons were given short shrift. An applicant never knew what the decision would be. What decision would you have made for each of these early applicants? A conscientious objector said he objected to military service which involved taking a life, and, as a lay preacher, he said it would lie upon his conscience for the rest of his life. He did not object to others fighting to save him but would take no reprisal if bombs fell and killed those around him. His application was refused. A clerk claiming he was unfit for service and had a doctor's note was told to see an army doctor for a check-up. And whilst a man with sole management responsibility for 12,000 acres was refused, a married painter with a number of contracts to fulfil was given six months' exemption.

It was the same across the country. A Bradford tribunal gave total exemption to a twenty-two stone man who said he was too heavy to fight. 'In fact,' he said, 'it takes me all my time to walk about.' Another tribunal could have easily told him that the army would do him good, what with all the fresh air, exercise and a healthy diet.

The army did not always play by the rules either. At the Hull tribunal, an Anlaby farmer applied to have his wagonner returned. While applying for his exemption they hustled him off to Beverley Barracks. As there was then no-one to feed the horses or set a rig, the appeal was allowed and the military were told to return the youth to his employer.

Even fairly obvious candidates for exemption might only be given a short time, and that usually in order to find someone else, whom the army did not want, to do their job. Such men were given a period of exemption and then allowed to apply again or not. A typical example of such an application was made by a young married man with one child, four horses, two wagonettes and a cart. He was a sub-contractor for the NER Company and for the Post Office, which used him for delivering mail. The written contract with the railway company had started forty years ago with his grandfather, who was now eighty-seven and his grandmother, who was ninety. On Saturday,

Those too young, too old, in poor health or a reserved occupation could still defend their country if the enemy invaded. A very youthful member of the East Yorkshire Volunteer Regiment.

they delivered twenty sacks of mail. Somewhat unsympathetically, all the Chairman of the tribunal was interested in was whether his grandfather was retiring from the job. As the applicant did not know, he was granted exemption until October and told he could apply again.

Sometimes a member of the tribunal tried to be a little too clever but, regardless, they had the last word. A father applied for his son to be exempted because he had two acres of garden and could not do without his son. The garden was his own, and he had two houses. Major Gosschalk, a tribunal member, tried to be clever with his opening remark that fell when the father replied. 'Couldn't you convert it into a poultry farm?' Appellant replied he had a lot of poultry and had sold 6,000 eggs and reared 1,000 chickens so far in 1916, and couldn't manage alone. The application was dismissed but the son was given a month before he was called up.

Hull's second air raid occurred on 5 March, only days after a table

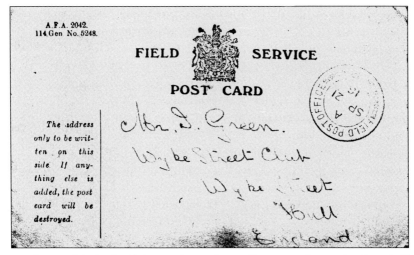

Mr Green of the Wyke Club was obviously a well-respected man. Another Field Service card to him but from a different sender.

of predicted dates for raids by the baby killers, as Zeppelins had come to be called because of their indiscriminate bombing of industrial and civilian targets had appeared in the papers. The table was based on new moons which gave sufficient light for them to find their target. High winds, storms and other weather would affect the likelihood of a raid but could, of course, not be predicted.

During this raid two Zeppelins, *L11* and *L 14*, hovered over the city for an hour. Their bombs caused extensive damage in the Queen Street and Collier Street areas, the glass roof of Paragon Station being destroyed. Seventeen people died and 60 were injured. Considerable damage was caused. The bombing 'destroyed houses, broke water mains, set fire to the Mariners' Almshouses, and to a shed on the docks. No guns or planes defended the town. The helpless population, in ugly mood, relieved its feelings by stoning a Royal Flying Corps vehicle in Hull, and a flying officer was mobbed in nearby Beverley.'

The next day the *Hull Daily Mail* carried a special correspondent's report on the incident. 'Searchlights flashed across the sky. Two great beams…immediately "found" the visitor. Simultaneously guns were put in action, and shells were seen to burst with surprising rapidity all round the object, which, still held in the rays of the searchlights, gleamed like a yellowish incandescent mantle. Shells burst with blinding flashes…the airship descended quickly to a low altitude, rose again and suddenly made out to sea.'

On 8 March, the *Hull Daily Mail* reported on the inquests on fifteen victims, six men, four women and five children, casualties of 5 March. The coroner presumed that their deaths were caused by the 'atrocious air raid' which had taken placed the previous day. He said that all who had suffered would receive consideration. Provision would be made for proper burial, and those who had lost furniture would be recompensed. Everything possible would be done for those who had suffered.

The stories told were very sad. The first witness, describing the death of her husband, told how the building fell on top of them. On scrambling out of the rubble she found her husband dead. A caretaker described how they had attempted to rescue an eighty-nine-year-old from the flames in his bedroom. Another inquest concerned three sisters. The bomb demolished most of their house, leaving the father, who had been in bed, to find one of his daughters dead and the other two lying on the ground, fatally injured.

A pathetic story was told by a mother, the wife of a fish fryer, whose eight-year-old son was killed. She had taken him and other children into the street thinking it would be safer. However, while they were walking, they were hit by bomb fragments. They were all knocked down. She and one child got up; her son was dead. A sixty-three-year-old man was found under debris wrapped in bedclothes. He was killed in his sleep. A wife described how her husband had gone to find out whether the safety buzzer was likely to be sounded. After that she knew nothing about what happened to him.

An especially sad story was the death of a mother and her four children, two boys and two girls, aged eight, six, four and two. The bomb had levelled their house and only the father survived. In the Commons, the government expressed their sympathy with relatives of the killed.

Showing any form of light after dark, for fear of guiding raiders to their targets, was prohibited by DORA regulations and strictly enforced by fines. Extinguishing lights regulations also included no bonfires after dark, especially during an air raid alarm date. On Northgate in Cottingham, on the night of 1 April, Samuel Johnson, a labourer, failed

The Zeppelin's Fight, Fright & Flight.

Twas on a Wednesday evening, April 5th,
  The cresent moon shone bright,
When Commander of ..L
  To England came to fight?
He took the old familiar track
  To the town he so well knew,
Where he'd slain the aged, the women folk,
  And suckling babies too.
He sailed quitely to the outskirts,
  About to make a dash ;
But terror seized on his black heart,
  As he met the search lights flash.
Just then the guns began to bark,
  And he fairly lost his head—
"O, Emperor, dear ! what shall I do ?
  In agony he said.
"Two times, before, I bravely cam e,
  In the witching hour of night,
Killed some women and children,
  And put the rest to flight.
It cannot be the babies
  Or the women fired that gun ;
They must have got some soldiers here ;
  It's time for me to run.
I thought all the men where soldiers,
  And the soldiers were away ;
And that the women and the babes
  I could the devil play.
They're cowardly inhuman,
  For they want to take my life—
These wicked, cruel Englishmen
  Are always starting strife.
Mine Gott ! who ruleth over hell,
  How can I get away?
If I get safely home again,
  I'll do my best to stay.

A postcard poem sold after the April 1916 raid.

to extinguish the bonfire at his cottage. For this oversight he was fined 15s because it 'cast a reflection for a considerable distance.'

On the night of 5 April, Edward Sutton was fined 9s. His crime? Striking a match on the Ferriby Road before 10 o'clock on the night of an alarm. An attempted raid that night was not successful.

In the same session at the Magistrates Court, several breaches of the lighting orders, at Hessle, Cottingham and elsewhere, were dealt with. Mrs Briggs of Hessle was fined 40s; William Jackson was fined 30s; William Harland and Thomas Smith were both fined 25s.

Sometimes it was a case of damned if you do and damned if you don't. Edward George, a Cottingham grocer and a volunteer dispatch rider, rode his motor cycle, without lights, on the night of 5 April, under the orders of a Special Constable. As a result he collided with a cart. Fortunately the magistrate understood the regulations, and while he castigated the specials for issuing the orders, he respited judgement on payment of costs.

The next raid occurred in the early hours of 9 August. 'Kapitänleutnant Koch, commanding *L24*, attacked the north-western parts of the city with twelve explosive and then thirty-one incendiary bombs. He then left in a northerly direction. The neighbourhoods around Selby Street bore the brunt of the attack that resulted in nine dead and around twenty wounded. Government advice was to take cover during a raid. Not heeding this advice was fatal for two of the Bearpark family of 35 Selby Street. A bomb dropped in the middle of the road opposite Mary Bearpark's house. She was standing near the doorway, and her daughter, Emma, rushed out of a neighbour's house. Both were killed. The boy and the father in the house were injured.'

Hull was lucky the next time the Zeppelins arrived. On 3 September the attack was driven off. It was nearly a year before they returned.

Mention has been made of the uncertainty involved in a seafarer's life. This is clearly shown by what happened to the Danish steamer *Vidar*, a neutral ship that had left Copenhagen for Hull. It had disappeared while crossing the North Sea. Actually it had been seized by a German destroyer and taken to Swinemünde in Germany. When it was released, its thirty passengers and her cargo of butter, eggs and milk were allowed to continue to Hull.

The figures for non-combatant losses at sea, reported by Mr Runciman in Parliament, showed how cities like Hull contributed to the war effort. Losses between 8 August 1914 and 15 April 1916 were 1,754 seamen, 183 fishermen and 1,175 passengers.

Mention has previously been made of the three constants in life in wartime Hull: change, petty crime and death. Death did not come only to military personnel and civilians through enemy action, but also through disease, old age and suicide, of which there were two unsuccessful and one successful attempts. John Keech and Aaron

Clixby were charged in separate incidents for trying to cut their throats. No reason was given for their behaviour, and nothing other than an unsound mind could be determined for William Gray's suicide. The fifty-three-year-old waggon inspector, employed by the Lancashire and Yorkshire Railway, who lived at 27 Cambridge Street, committed suicide by attaching a tube from the gas jet to his mouth. Although he had been out of work for six months, he had no financial problems and was not depressed. Complaining he could not sleep, he sent his wife to get a sleeping draught. On return she found him dead with a pipe in his mouth attached to the gas meter.

As for petty crimes, there were pig killers. In March, twelve-year-old Joseph Barnes was accused of killing a pig and remanded because he had three previous convictions.

Some families were more affected than others by death. On 11 April, the widow Mrs A.E. Moody, of 48 St Andrew Street, Hessle Road, lost her third son in the war. Her son Benjamin was serving with the 3rd East Yorkshires at Beverley when he died.

For a range of reasons, soldiers did not always give their correct name or address and sometimes either or both were recorded incorrectly. In June, Mrs Hall of 10 Alfred Street, received a letter to Mr Webster or Kelly with her address on it. It had been wrongly addressed. The envelope contained a letter from a Second Lieutenant, the CO of No.3 section, 92 Brigade MG Company, dated 29 May 1916. 'I deeply regret to inform you that your son, Number 28121 Private James Webster was killed on Saturday last, the 27th inst., during a bombardment of our HQ. He was a good soldier, and a man I very sincerely regret losing. Please accept my heartfelt sympathy in your bereavement.' Naturally Mrs Hall wanted to get the letter to his parents but whether she did was not stated. It is unlikely, as he had obviously enlisted under an alias with a false address.

As in other parts of the country, stories of patriotic families helped to show how everyone was pulling together. One such family were the Cutsforths who had six serving or who had served: Tom, invalided out after the Aisne fighting on 24 September 1914; George in the Royal Field Artillery was serving in France (he had previously been with W.C. Bell in Market Place); Ted, a sergeant in the RAMC, employed by Sutton's in Prince Street, had re-joined at the start of the war; Frederick, a driver with the ASC in France, was employed by R. Field and son in

Saville Street; Joseph, serving with a territorial battalion of the Lincolnshire Regiment in France, was an employee of the Great Central Railway (GCR) on Grimsby Docks; a brother-in-law Lance Corporal M.J. Steele had been killed in action in Belgium in May 1915 serving with the 4th East Yorkshires.

Not all the news was negative. Two young ladies resident in Hull undertook farm work near Harrogate for four months. They had been provided with excellent accommodation. The story was a recruitment appeal in disguise. Girls were wanted 'who were not afraid of work to join them in their effort to do their bit in the country's emergency.' They made the point that with wages at 15s a week, enough to cover expenses and food, the work was not for those who wanted to make a profit. It was a purely patriotic gesture and 'an excellent chance for the daughters of gentlemen within the city…[to] release…more men to fight the Huns. Application forms from the recruiting office at City Hall.'

As today, stories involving the Royal Family were popular, even if there was only a small link to home. In April the King inspected trawlers, drifters and patrol boats at Garleston and Great Yarmouth. He boarded one small drifter and conversed with the skipper, Captain Stoners of 57b Anlaby Road, who before the war had sailed for Messrs Pickering and Haldane as captain of the trawler *T.R. Ferens.*

Previous mention of trawlers has shown that an already hard life was made even harder by the Germans. On the positive side for those still fishing, things had improved by Easter 1916. 'Admiralty arrangements made it possible for a small composite fleet of steam

A silk marker commemorating Private Banning. Once a common object most have been thrown away and those remaining are fragile with age.

In Remembrance
OF
PRIVATE,
George Dugdall Banning,
Who Died of Wounds received in Action in France,
July 4th, 1916.
Aged 22 Years.

Interred St. Severs Cemetery, Rouen.

Not now but in the coming years,
It may be in the better land,
We'll read the meaning of our tear
And there sometime we'll understand.

270, St. Georges Road, Hull.

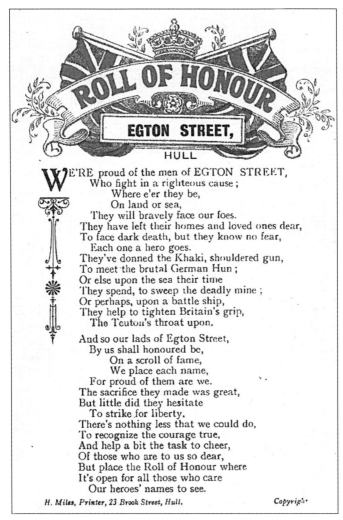

Many streets set up a shrine for those serving and/or those who had been killed. Egton Street also produced a postcard about their men and shrine.

trawlers to work in a comparatively safe area at a considerable profit. Record after record was made, and the share system employed on board provided a good living for skippers and mates. In April 1916, a few days before Good Friday, when fish was scarce, the Hull trawler *Elf King* landed a catch worth £3,670 (the previous record had been £3,480 held by the same trawler). This gave the skipper a wage of £300 [£5,000 today] and made him a rich man.'

'While those still fishing were making money, the reduction in the number of vessels meant a corresponding decrease in wealth for fisher-girls who lost their traditional occupations of "gipping" and packing. They moved into munitions, postal work and other employment, but most of them found it hard to match the standard of living they had been used to.' Even so, most still dug into their pockets for Flag Days.

A successful Flag Day was good news and showed how generous the city was. The YMCA Flag Day at the end of March raised £693 3s 2d. However, after two years, although they continued to give, many were bored with them as a contemporary joke showed. 'Man: "Oh! I'm sick of these flag days." Maid: "Well I hope the soldiers won't get sick of fighting for you".'

The Hull Gift Day around the same time was also an unqualified success. Gifts poured in all day at the Guildhall and Peel House and included donations of 184 tins of meat, 386 tins of fish, 35 tins of soup, 8 bottles of coffee, 51 tins of tooth powder, 88 tins of mints, 6 New Testaments, 224 tins of Vaseline, 9 boxes of bars of chocolate, 28 boxes of cigarettes, 10 boxes of tobacco, 33 boxes of matches, 2 packets of postcards, 2 writing pads, 3 hussifs (housewives – a small sewing kit) and cash totalling £23 14s 1d.

Not everyone who joined the army was an enthusiastic soldier. Men might desert or disappear, some successfully, others for a short time. Two such men were William Harrison and William Gray, both of Hull. In May they appeared at the Magistrates Court charged with being deserters from the Army Reserve. 'The two men had been living for four or five weeks in a fishing smack belonging to Harrison on the river Trent. Gray had a munition workers badge and certificate obtained while working at Earle's ship building works, which he left on 24 March but failed to give up his badge. It was an obvious case of evasion of military duty the chairman told the court. He fined each 40s and remanded them while they waited for an escort.'

There was another manhunt in September. The Yorkshire Wolds were scoured in September by the East Riding police for an unnamed man who was thought to be evading military service. He was traced to the River Derwent and later sent them word that they had been only two yards away from him when a sergeant was searching the river

Pte. C. ROSE.   Pte. C. W. MARTIN.   Pte. W. McKERNAN.   Corp. L. PEEK.

C. J. PEASEGOOD.   L.-C. W. MALTBY.   Pte. H. E. BOXHALL.   Pte. J. PAGE.

Official intimation has been received of the death of Private Charles Rose, East Yorkshire Regiment, which occurred in France last month. Before joining the Army a few months after the outbreak of war he was employed at the National Radiator Company's works. His home is at 21, Wellsted-street, Hull, and he leaves a widow and three young children to mourn his loss.

News has been received of the death of Private Geo. W. Martin (19), 711, East Yorks., who has been killed in action. He was the son of Mr George Martin, 14, Parrott-street. In a letter to the mother the acting commanding officer writes:—"Private Martin was killed at his post in the firing line on May 26th during a bombardment of some severity, in which our company suffered considerable loss. After all, Private Martin died doing his duty in a place of danger, and I know of no better tribute to a soldier's memory." The chaplain (Rev E. F. Habershon) also writes a sympathetic letter, in which he states that he conducted the funeral with several of his comrades, who died at the same time, and a cross has since been erected over the grave.

Pte. W McKernan, E. Yorks, 157, Buckingham-street, who is reported to have died of wounds received in action, Company Sergt.-Major H. C. Cooke, in a letter to the mother, writes:—"We are all sorry to lose him. He always did his best and was always willing, and you have the consolation, poor in some ways but great in others, of knowing that, although young, he died a man's death, doing his duty to his country. He was buried in a brigade cemetery, with a party of D Company to pay their last respects."

Lance-Corpor'l J. Lewis Peek, East Yorks, is officially reported to have been killed in action on June 4th. Sergeant Hall, in charge of the platoon, in a sympathetic letter to the mother, Mrs Peek, 88, Summergangs-road, states that her son was struck by a piece of shell during a heavy bombardment in the early hours of June 4th, and that he died instantly, without any suffering whatever. The writer adds:—"I always found him ready and willing to do anything that was asked of him. He was one of my most capable

and reliable N.C.O.'s, and will be very much missed by myself and his section. He did his duty, and died the death of a true Britisher at his post. We buried him the same night in a military cemetery behind the line." He was 23 years of age. A brother, Lieut. Arnold Peek, is on active service in the Navy.

Cyril John Peasegood, East Yorks., who was well known on the Hull cars, was killed in action on the 26th ult., and was the fourth son of the late John Wilkinson Peasegood, of Australia, grandson of the late William Peasegood, oil merchant, of Hull, who was Sheriff of this city, and for some years chairman of the Kingston Gas Company. The deceased has two brothers now serving, one in the Navy and one in the 9th Yorks, who is wounded, and the grandson of the late Foster William Lester, of Swanland Dale, sergeant-major of the Prince of Wales's Own (West Yorkshire Regiment). Mr Peasegood was 23 years of age; was married, and has left a widow and young child, whose home is at Hull.

Lance-Corporal Wilfrid Maltby, Royal Highlanders of Canada, killed on or about April 22nd, 1915. He was eight years in Canada previous to joining the forces, and came over with the first forces from Canada. He was a well-known Hull bricklayer, residing at 6, Selkirk-street, Hull, before leaving for Canada.

Private H. C. Boxhall, E.Y.R., killed in a heavy bombardment in France on May 26th. Before joining he was a seaman on board the Wilson liner s.s. Oslo for years. He has left a widow and five children. His home was at 10, Granville-terrace, Strickland-street, Hessle-road, Hull. He was one of those whom Private Brett (whose photograph was published recently in the "Mail") made a gallant attempt to rescue. Letters of sympathy have been received by Mrs Boxhall from his colonel and chaplain, both of whom speak in the highest terms of his courage and tenacity.

Private James Page, King's Royal Rifles, of 3, Sarah's-terrace, Alexandra-street, Hull, who is reported to have died in France of wounds on May 26. He had been on active service twelve months, and would have been 18 on July 5th.

Details of local losses before the battle of the Somme started.

Prisoners of War at Ruhleben.

Among them are officers and seamen from Hull and Grimsby who will be easily recognised. On the right of the photograph, second row, is First Officer J. W. Forton, s.s. Coralie Horlock, who has been a prisoner since the outbreak of war.

Mrs Forton, 39, Belvoir-street, wishes, through the "Mail," to thank Mr Barclay for bringing her the information as to her husband. Mr Barclay has received kindnesses from Mr Forton during Mr Barclay's illness at the camp, for which he is grateful. Mr Barclay, whose present address is 7, Windser-crescent, Bridlington, was released from the internment camp through illness To recognise Mr Forton's kindness Mr Barclay has called on Mrs Forton and has left with her a parcel as a gift to be forwarded to Mr Forton at the Ruhleben Camp. Mrs Forton also wishes to thank the "Mail" for assistance in finding her address.

Captured merchant seamen were not combatants and were housed in a civilian PoW camp at Ruhleben. The photograph shows a group of Hull seamen in captivity.

bank. The man was living on turnips and sleeping under stooks of corn. As on other occasions, the paper did not follow up the story and the reader was left with no answer.

People relied upon the papers for truthful news, but they certainly did not get it about the start of the Somme offensive. Readers were told by the *Hull Times,* published that day, that the offensive had begun with

THE   HULL   TIMES,   APRIL   29,   1916.——6

At Ruhleben : Do you Know Them ?

All E. Riding and Hull men captured by the Germans on August 29th, 1914—the first month of the war—from trawlers in the North Sea. The faces will be recognised, doubtless, by our readers. We cannot give the names of all these men, but are assured that many familiar Hull faces are among the group. For instance the one in the middle of the third row in front in white jersey—is Mr J. C. Dunn, 58, Railway Cottages, Dairycoates. They are all looking very well. The figure on the left of the photo in morning dress and an armlet on is a Grimsby man.
A photo of another group of local men, prisoners of war at the Ruhleben Camp, appears in the "*Sports Mail.*"

A football team at Ruhleben made up of Hull and East Riding trawler men captured in August 1914.

an attack on a twenty mile front. The fighting was furious; many prisoners were taken as well as the German front line. 'Our casualties are not heavy.' The assaults were preceded by a bombardment of 1½ hours. What did they think when the casualty lists were released?

With the realisation that manpower was limited, in July the government finally recognised the Volunteer Force. It was given a specific role in the event of invasion; to guard strategic points and hinder the advance, adding to its job of active coastal patrols. Now it was part of the Armed Forces, members had to drill at least ten times in a month.

Most city tramways made handsome profits during the war, which allowed them to subsidise other departments. Hull also had the only independent telephone installation in the country. In the year ending in July, it had made a gross operating profit of £56,228 against £23,250 the previous year. Its net profit was £3,645, even though the number of subscribers had dropped. After the war there were plans to extend the system.

As Hull was a port, ships and shipping stories occurred regularly. Representative stories included a Hull man in ice, a careless Danish captain, vegetables for the fleet, the loss of the SS *Thurso* and the tonnage of goods landed in Hull.

What was a Hull man doing stuck in ice? He was part of the crew of a ship frozen in at Archangel. To pass the time they organised, with help from the port chaplain and ladies of the consulate, a concert to raise money for Russian wounded. Smoking was not allowed in the concert room and those who did were fined and given the order of the 'Crossed Matches'. The concert raised £150 and the fines were used to pay for cigarettes, papers and tobacco for Russian soldiers. Matches were in the news for another reason shortly after this story. It was no longer possible to send matches through the post. Too many had burst into flames and much mail was lost by the fires caused.

Why would a neutral sea captain fall foul of the law? As had happened to Hull skipper James Elliot at Milford Haven in 1915, it was a captain who did not know the DORA regulations. Captain Thomsen

The staff of a small engineering work in Beverley. By 1916 most employees were women. Note the triangular badge worn signifying employment on war work.

was fined £75 plus costs or six months' imprisonment for his lights. Between 11.30 pm and 2.30 am he had permitted outboard lights, other than those required by regulation, to be visible.

Built in 1909 and owned by the Wilson Line, the SS *Thurso* was bringing timber from Archangel to Hull when she was captured by *U44*, under the command of Captain Paul Wagenführ. Except for the captain and first engineer, the crew were allowed to leave the ship before it was sunk by gunfire. One of the crew, C.J. Kibble, came from Hull.

Hull Corn Trade Association reported wheat imports for the month ended 31 August. Amounts were down on the previous month and year; 164,903 quarters of wheat were imported at Hull compared with 210,329 in July and 306,243 in August 1915.The imports for wheat for the year to September were 1,691,722 quarters compared with 2,893,488 in the corresponding period of 1915. It was the same for maize, nearly 60,000 quarters less than 1915, but not for barley imports which had increased considerably since 1915. Other commodities showed the same pattern. It was obvious that everyone would be facing some form of rationing if imports kept falling.

Then there were the elements to deal with. Lightning was unpredictable and dangerous. During the first days of September there was a terrific thunderstorm over parts of the East Riding. A youth at a solicitor's desk suffered cuts to the hands and face as glass flew from a window struck by lightning. A horse struck by lightning was killed, though the rider was unharmed. Lightning struck five draught horses standing in a line in a field, killing them all, while in some areas considerable damage was wrought on standing corn.

Although little was mentioned about the bane of rising prices, constant shortages guaranteed this would apply to even humble foods like the potato. Blight had hit the potato harvest, resulting in short supply and steadily rising prices. The crop from Scotland was particularly badly hit. Prices were £9-£10 a ton, with transport adding a further 35s. This was against a pre-war norm of £3-£4 in autumn and in 1915 £6 a ton was classed as a fair price.

Flour also went up in price. By August the cost of flour had increased by 2s to 54s 6d. Double Super No.1 Manitoba wheat had cost 48s 6d on 26 June; on 12 August it was 70s. Naturally wages failed to keep up with the price rises.

Fortunately the harvest was good in quantity and quality so prices would not rise too quickly. To make sure the East Riding harvest was brought in, it was necessary to release soldiers to assist, but, as many of the men released were not agricultural workers, it was not as smooth a harvest as it could have been.

Brief notes about unit movements or awards appeared regularly, even if not from Hull. Private Chafer, from Bradford, was serving with 1st Battalion East Yorkshire Regiment when he won the Victoria Cross. At a less exalted level of bravery, Sapper Smith of 15 Kelvin Street, employed at H&B Co engineers department was acknowledged for winning the Military Medal (MM) and being promoted to Lance Corporal. Six months after the event, the 11th Hull Heavy Battery was reported to have arrived at Kilindini Port in Kenya.

Throughout the war, loved ones who fell, husbands and sons, were remembered in the death notices. Some were poetic, macabre, some asked for understanding, others were simple statements of loss. It is also interesting to note how many of the fathers had predeceased their sons. The following are representative. 'Charles. Killed in action September 10th Henry Walter, the dearly-loved son of the late John and Louise Charles aged 36.

A sudden change;
I in a short time fell
And had not time to bid my friends farewell;
Think it not strange, death happens unto all;
My lot today;
Tomorrow you may fall.'

'Davey. August 9th 1916 Killed in action, Sergeant Hamlet Davey, dearly-loved son of Mrs and the late Mr Davey, 34 Dover Street, aged 37.
We often think of him,
And think of how he died;
To think he could not say goodbye,
Before he closed his eyes;
When days are dark and friends are few,
'Tis then, dear Hamlet, we think of you – Deeply mourned by his loving mother, brothers, and sister, also friends.'

'Allenby.   September 8th 1916 Killed in action, Private George Allenby, aged 25 and Lance-Corporal W. T. Allenby, aged 20 of the Canadians, dearly loved sons of Ellen and the late David Allenby.
Greater love hath no man than this, that a man lay down his life for his friends.'

'Billett. Killed in action September 15th, Private George Herbert, beloved husband of Frances, aged 36 years. R.I.P.'

'Emerson. Killed in action September 10th 1916, Private H Emerson, beloved son of Elizabeth and the late Charles, 9, Kingston Place, Witham. Someday we'll understand.'

Christmas was fast approaching and organising treats for men on active service took a lot of time and effort. The Christmas pudding One Shilling Fund started in October. The money was collected in conjunction with *The Daily Telegraph* and *London Daily News* to provide the East Yorkshire Regiment with puddings. Men from Hull in other units would receive theirs through a national fund which stood at 126,970 shillings. This was a lot of Christmas puddings as 2s 6d

Hedon was an equine centre for the army. Here horses are being loaded for onward transport.

provided enough for five men, one guinea for fifty and £1 11s 6d for a platoon. Douglas Haig added his voice to the appeal. 'On behalf of those whose Christmas will be made brighter by your kindness, I wish to thank you.' £60,000 was wanted. At that time Hull had contributed a mere 97½ shillings but, by early December, the city had raised 9,000 shillings. By Christmas, Lord Burnham was able to thank the *Hull Daily Mail* and the *Hull Times* for the £535 19s 6d they had raised, providing puddings for 25,000 local "lads" all over the world.

Competing for money and food at the same time was another charity, Vegetables for the Fleet (and Minesweepers). It had sent over 600 cases in six months, all bought from the New Market in Hull.

With food becoming scarcer, many in Hull wanted to rent an allotment. Unfortunately, demand was greater than supply. The problem was partially solved, as in other towns and cities, by purchasing, renting or loaning land. In addition to allotments on Hedon Road, Portobello Street, Cottingham Road, Southcoates, Perth Street and Mill Lane, Hull Corporation took the decision to rent land in a number of areas: twelve acres at the foot of Middleburg Street; Steynburg Street near New Bridge Road; eighteen acres at the back of property at Exmouth Street; and Cottingham Drain.

For the poor, many things were in short supply. At the end of October, the Hull Children's Clothing Fund held its annual meeting. It reported that it had supplied the poor children of Hull with 112 pairs of boots, three pairs of clogs and 115 pairs of stockings, while a further 250 children received other articles of clothing.

As with individuals, some companies prospered while others in the same line did not. In late 1916, the Wilson Line of Hull, doubtless prompted by the loss of three of its largest and most prestigious vessels to enemy action – *Aaro*, the first ship on the Humber to carry wireless, and *Calypso*, both sunk, and *Eskimo,* captured during a three-week period in the summer – was sold to Sir John Ellerman, owner of the Ellerman Line.

Towards the end of the year, the fourth murder of the war happened off Hessle Road. Seventeen-year-old Jack Gibbons fatally stabbed his father at their home, 58 Wassand Street. Mother and father were arguing when Jack intervened and stabbed him in the windpipe with his pocket knife. He was sent to the assizes on the reduced charge of manslaughter.

Around the same time, Dr Sidney Firth, of Grantham, was charged at the Police Court with the murder of Emma Shaw, the thirty-nine-year-old wife of a dairy manager of St George's Road. At the inquest in November, the verdict had been death due to septicaemia caused by an abortion, but there was no evidence to show how it was caused. Bail was refused and the case was to continue in the New Year.

The third Christmas of the war was not a season of goodwill. Hull Tramways started the season by deciding that, although it had made a £12,000 profit, it was necessary to abolish the ½d fare. And, despite being short of manpower, it was still not prepared to have women drivers. In a season noted for excess, the mayor asked for temperance in everything.

In its Christmas issue, the *Hull Times* wished its readers, 'in the trenches, in the camps, in billets, on the high seas, at home and all over the world, as Happy Christmas as the times permit, and trusts fervently that Christmas 1917 will see the restoration of peace.'

Christmas is traditionally a time for giving. In the PoW camp in Salserbad, Captain Stanley Wilson MP, King's Messenger, wrote a letter to his solicitors. He instructed them to send a cheque for £200 to the Lord Mayor of Hull and £50 to the Mayor of Beverley for distribution amongst local charities.

For some it would a happier time than for others. The bravery of some local men was noted in the papers. Reverend Saxelbye-Evers, pre-war curate of St Matthew's Church, had been awarded the Military Cross (MC) for caring for or carrying wounded men for eighteen hours from No-Man's Land. Other Hull men singled out were Privates James Dixon and E. Kirby, Sergeants Bulmer, P.W. Griggs, S. Stonehouse and R. Ward, who were awarded the MM and Sergeant A. Clare and Corporal W. Moore who were awarded a bar to their MM.

For some the season was a time of great sadness. On 15 December, Lieutenant Reginald Gaskell, the only son of a Hull councillor, was killed in a flying accident. He had joined the colours in September 1914, been commissioned, served in France, transferred to the Royal Flying Corps (RFC) and flown on the Western Front for eight months as an observer before returning to England to train as a pilot. He was twenty-seven.

At least the Gaskells had closure. For many, a loved one was listed as missing. Some accepted the situation. Others asked for information

With ever increasing numbers of Hull prisoners the packing room for PoW goods became a very busy place.

like the parents of nineteen-year-old Corporal Piper, who had been missing since 13 November, and the family of Private Newborn, who had been missing since 7 November. It was not only the families of soldiers who wanted news. On Boxing Day, another nineteen-year-old, Lily Edwards, went missing, not on the Western Front, but from 55 Norwood Grove in Beverley. Naturally, her parents were also very anxious for any news.

There were further restrictions coming in the New Year that would affect everyone. It was reported that the future would see meatless days when it would be unlawful to buy, sell or eat meat anywhere – this, though, would not apply to fish. Other changes to which the population of Hull would not look forward included sugar rationing, a savings programme on potatoes to ensure sufficient were available for next year's crop, restrictions on flour production from maize, oats and barley, and, very seriously, less tea because of reduced shipping space. More positively, steps were to be taken to increase the number of pigs, because, like potatoes, they were an important part of the working class diet. In the New Year, regulations would be relaxed to allow people to apply to have a pig-sty on their land in Hull in the same way as was already permitted at Cottingham Castle.

To help families get through the meatless day, a competition was run for recipes and menus that would be nutritious but meatless. Mrs

Featherstone, of 20 Suffolk Street, and Mrs Hanslip, of 5 Curson Street, each won 5s for their recipes. There were many suggestions of which these are a few: Breakfast – fried tomatoes on toast, Dinner – 3d of bones, 1d large turnip, 1d of onions, 2d of carrots, flavoured with pepper and salt and simmered for three hours, Tea – macaroni and tomatoes.

The need for money was unabated. Pre-Christmas appeals came from the National Egg Collection that urgently needed more eggs for the wounded, and the Interned Hull Seaman's War Charity. Although it had raised £725 19s 5d with a Flag Day, donations and gifts, it had outgoings of £25 a week and more was still needed. It also urgently needed gifts of boots and clothes to send to Germany.

There was also a need for local charity. The Mother Humber Fund helped the poor

Harold Cook, the writer's maternal grandfather, a sixteen-year-old Hull factory worker. Two years later he would be wearing khaki.

and aged in the area with visits and financial assistance and reported on those it helped. One East Hull lady member came across a poor woman without either food or fire who 'did not know what to do.' Her husband had been injured at work and she had been told to wait to be attended to in due time. She was provided temporary help by the fund. At another house the husband was ill with TB. The wife worked very hard and had two boys whom she was bringing up respectably. The fund assisted. On Holderness Road they helped an eighty-three-year-old widow who had worked in a tailor's shop until she was eighty-one and was surviving on 5s a week. To December the fund had issued thirteen 1s grocery orders, 301 2s grocery orders and 425 coal orders to local needy people.

The third Christmas of the war was one of austerity but nevertheless, in the institutions, everyone tried to make the most of what they had or could get. The children in the scarlet fever ward had a visit from Father Christmas, who distributed gifts from the tree. For entertainment the staff performed sketches and dialogues, and everyone sang carols and songs. Father Christmas also visited the diphtheria, enteric and isolation wards.

A Photo from Germany.

Private E. Mail, husband of Mrs Mail, of 24, Green-lane, Hull, has been a prisoner of war for 14 months in Germany. He is in the King's Own Scottish Borderers, and is the third figure to the left in the photo, which he has sent his wife from Germany. Before being called up he was a lamplighter for the British Gas Light Co., Baker-street. Note the German officer on guard, with fixed bayonet, on the right.

Private Mail of Green Lane sent this photo home from Germany. It is unclear which he is but as two of the men are German, one Russian and the other French or Belgian, he is probably the taller man in the centre.

At Reckitt's Social Hall, then a newly-authorised military hospital, patients had a very enjoyable Christmas tree party with Mrs Philip Reckitt distributing hundreds of presents. In the evening there was a whist drive and dance. Throughout the war the men in the hospital were so well looked after that it became the hospital that men wished to get into if they could.

At the Anlaby Road workhouse, inmates were provided with Christmas dinner of roast beef, potatoes, plum pudding and sauce. They were visited by the Lord Mayor and his wife. He left a three-penny piece for every child, 1oz of tobacco for each man and 4oz of tea for each woman. In Park Avenue Industrial School for girls, the visitors included not only the Lord and Lady Mayor but the Sheriff as well. Industrial schools were intended to solve problems of juvenile delinquency, by removing poor and neglected children from their home environment to a boarding school. Magistrates were allowed to send disorderly children to a residential industrial school. It was reported that the girls looked a picture of health and contentment and that the Lord Mayor addressed them with words of encouragement and hope. When the guests left they were heartily cheered at the request of the matron. This was not the end of the day's pleasure for the boarders. 'Every hour was crowned with joy and gladness and the climax came when, with the assistance of matron and her staff, they organised an impromptu concert, the items of which were interspersed with parlour games. Then before the order to retire was given the school rang with hearty cheers for those who had contributed to probably the happiest Christmas Day spent in the school.'

The Reverend Guttery, leader of the Primitive Methodists, expressed the feelings of most people. 'Christmas and the New Year will seem strange without you. We miss you more than we dare tell. Our family parties are broken, our glee is shadowed, though we shall still keep smiling, for that is what you would have us do. Santa Claus will not seem to the little children quite the jovial old party he used to be. You would not like the youngsters to go without their gifts, and we will keep the stockings full. War economy must not starve love ... Our girls are very lonely, but they are brave. You need not be afraid – not one of them will give up the boy in the trenches or on board ship for the boy who has stayed at home. We have no desire for feasting and parties this year, though we will not be doleful, for we would be worthy of your cheerful courage.'

Overall it was a lacklustre Christmas as the leader writer of the *Hull Times* wrote. 'The clear two days' rest this Christmas has been welcome to thousands of hard workers, though the customary festivities have been, in this third war Christmas, somewhat subdued. Leave for our soldier relatives could only be sparingly granted, but the men in khaki in Hull were largely compensated by the unselfish efforts at entertainment made by the well-disposed people...Beyond football there was little to induce people to leave their firesides.'

Besides it was difficult to get around as 'the tram service was

The third war Christmas and the Hull Times *once again sent its Christmas greetings around the world. This time it is hoping for peace before the next one.*

Hammond's moved to its present position in 1916. An advert for the clearance sale before it left its premises in Osborne Street.

suspended at 4.40 pm.' Hull was not unusual. 'Throughout the country the day was quiet.'

Sir Mark Sykes, the MP for Holderness, wrote to the people of Hull expressing why the country needed to keep fighting. 'To all of you who are suffering here at home and overseas in the cause of honesty, right and justice, I would say, in all humility, future generations yet unborn shall live to bless the courage, steadfastness, and patience of the British people, who lived in this time of chastisement and sorrow.'

How much consolation was gained from Sir Mark's words cannot be known. Perhaps it gave pause to think about personal losses in the wider scheme of things as the losses continued. Losses such as R.H. Foster, who died when the SS *Vasco* hit a mine in the Channel, and Fred Rodgers, of 12 Victoria Terrace, who was killed on a minesweeper. Could such words help the widow and child of John Waterman, 6 Park Avenue, (better known as Jack Rowntree after his grandfather who brought him up), a third hand on the trawler *Quair*? Or the widow and seven children of Thomas Delph, chief engineer on the *Quair*?

They may have meant more to the family of Edward Blythe, who was missing in action at the time. Unexpectedly they received a postcard telling them he had lost everything but was okay and not to worry.

How did Hull feel about the New Year? Just a week after a casualty list of 1¼ columns the editor had this to say. 'The end of a year is invariably a time for reflection...whilst we are ready to admit the possibility of the year upon which we hope soon to enter being the greatest year in the modern history of our Empire, it is equally true to say that 1916 was the point upon which turned its fate.'

There was a different message at the end of 1917.

G.D. Longfellow of 529 Field Company
before leaving for France in 1916.

CHAPTER 4

1917:
Seeing it Through

In Hull there was little to mark the coming of the New Year. It was the same in London where only a few lingered in the drizzling rain for the hour when night becomes morning. As in Hull, most people stayed home. With restaurants closed and no bells to chime there was little point in being out. 'A year of abounding hope could not have been ushered in more quietly or more soberly.'

The *Eastern Daily News* was more loquacious in its first editorial of the New Year. 'What a contrast to the ringing out of the Old and the ringing in of the New before the war cast its broad shadow of sorrow and bereavement over the world! The old year slipped away quietly, and 1917 came in just as quietly. True a few folk kept up the old custom of waiting in the city square until the New Year was born but it was a small crowd, and as quiet as it was small. No sirens screeched, no bells rang out, there was no booming of the fateful hour which marked the dividing line between the Old and the New…And so 1916 passed away with few regrets save for those who have gone with it, and 1917 was born with great expectation and hope.'

A journalist for the *Hull Daily Mail* recorded his thoughts on the first day of the New Year in the 1 January 1917 edition. 'On this New Year morning there is some blue in the sky; great events also mark the birth of 1917…Today a great number of Englishmen are called-up to the colours to take their part in our defence…The way women have come to the rescue is more noticeable now…the increase in fares on railway trains beginning today, will tend to reduce unnecessary travelling, though it will inconvenience those who have to make journeys. The increase of hair-cutting and shaving prices is another indication of the New Year.'

Would the New Year be any different? Was there anything to look forward to other than shortages and price increases? The stories in the papers suggest not.

The trial of Dr. Firth was adjourned for the second time with the defence claiming Emma Shaw had fallen from a tram or taken drugs, as there was no evidence of an instrument involved in an illegal operation. On the first day of the year, the troopship *Ivernia* sank with the loss of eighty-five soldiers and thirty-six crew members and, just before Christmas, the SS *Yarrowdale* had been captured at sea and taken to Germany where she became *Leopard* SS. Rail fare prices went up by thirty per cent and food was so short in some places that they were catching and cooking sparrows. The preferred recipe was in a 'lark pudding'.

Petty crime showed no sign of abating. A boy charged with stealing a door key was found also with a stolen watch. As he was already on probation he was sent to a Remand Home. For walking around the docks, a Russian sailor received fourteen days, while a Norwegian was given only ten for the same offence. An eleven-year-old boy was convicted of throwing a stone and breaking a bus window valued at 15s. The soldier whom he had also hit was uninjured. This was the second time he had done this. His mother said the boy was practically unmanageable and punishment was no deterrent. The President of the Court said he was a very bad boy and regretted that he could not order him whipped. Instead the parents were fined 30s to cover costs and the window. He hoped the parents would deal with him in a more effective manner in future.

Later in the year, an elderly man set a Hull record for offences. When John Borrill was found guilty of begging in Trinity Street it was stated that he had been before the court seventy-four times before. The best that the town of Reading could offer in competition was Charles Hamblin, who had appeared before the bench sixty-one times before he decided he wanted to be a soldier. Borrill's reason was simple: he 'had got very badly off', couldn't find work and had to beg. When he was seen going from door to door he had 1s 6d on him. He was sentenced to two months in prison.

The reason why there had been insufficient meat available in Hull was explained. It was simple; there had been a large decrease in the number of animals entering Hull cattle market during the year, down on 1915 by 20,153 head.

	1915	1916	Decrease
Cattle	32,696	31,578	1,098
Sheep	150,900	141,925	8,975
Pigs	41,186	31,106	10,080

On a positive note, the Hull and East Riding Voluntary Aid Committee thanked everyone for their donations which totalled £1,317 15s. This allowed it to send to local men a bar of chocolate, a packet of chewing gum and a tin of fifty cigarettes. In addition, comforts had been despatched to the various officers' and sergeants' messes, books and games had been forwarded to units in Salonika, Egypt, Bermuda, Mesopotamia and East Africa, and a specially produced journal *The Hull Searchlight*, 'full of local colouring (sic)' was sent to troops abroad. Gramophone records, playing cards, quoits, writing pads, envelopes, pencils, and other materials were issued to various troops where COs had made applications.

In the same vein, the Hull and East Riding Fund for the needs of local units and prisoners of war was also pleased with itself. It had raised over £5,000 between 7 August 1915 and September 1916, of which £2,000 had been raised by the Flag Day on 8 July. This had allowed it to send 38,221 articles of clothing out to the troops and 6,000 parcels to PoWs. During the same period, 15,360 articles had been received at the Lady Mayoress' depot in the Guildhall, of which 10,989 had been despatched.

Across the country, farmers had converted grassland into arable and increased the acreage for crops. In the East Riding the increase was marginal, so there would be shortfalls in production against consumption which could not be replaced by imports. However, in Hull the Mayor proudly reported that 650 acres were available for allotments with a further 240 more to be available in the neighbourhood of

Sidmouth Street and New Bridge Road. Unlike many towns and cities, Hull had enough land to meet demand.

There would be many appeals over the year. The first was for 1,000 pairs of socks for a battalion of the East Yorkshire Regiment. This was followed by a wider appeal to the country's patriotism and pockets.

To assist in the projected great push for the new war loan, special offices were opened in Lombard Street. Even before they opened they were besieged with requests for prospectuses. Evidence of the good deal they were perceived to be is shown by institutional purchase: Prudential £20,000,000; General Insurance Company £1,250,000; Guardian Assurance Company £350,000; Liverpool Corporation £1,000,000; Leeds Council £250,000. Even Hull Corporation found £100,000 to invest.

Two weeks later, to continue the momentum of the loan, a mass meeting was held at Queen's Hall, chaired by the mayor and addressed by Sir Edward Carson. The importance of the meeting is clearly shown by those attending who included the High Steward (Hon. T.R. Ferens), the Sheriff of Hull (A.J. Atkinson), Colonel Sir Mark Sykes MP, Sir Luke White MP, Colonel Sir Robert Aske, Sir Alfred Gelder MP, G.J. Bentham MP and the aldermen and councillors of the City. Lord Nunburnholme was too ill to attend.

Hull's target was to raise £3,000,000 in war loans. Within two days of the meeting, it had raised £3,560,000 with over £3,000,000 coming from Sir John Ellerman. When it closed on 17 February, £7,000,000 had been raised in just sixteen days.

There was some good news. Hull had become a sober city. The following table shows the number of convictions for drunkenness in English cities with more than 200,000 inhabitants.

Another member of the writer's extended family who did not return. Private Moses Atkinson was originally with the 14th Battalion. This photograph was taken when he was home on leave sometime after he was wounded in 1917. He was killed in action with the 7th Battalion East Yorkshire Regiment on 31 March 1918 at the age of twenty-one.

	1914	1915	1916
Greater London & City	57,634	51,836	29.453
Birmingham	3,746	2,309	1,332
Liverpool	12,289	9,155	5,836
Manchester	7,050	4,304	2,631
Sheffield	1,473	1,111	661
Leeds	1,730	1,236	617
Bradford	1,045	752	528
Hull	1,995	1,468	630
Newcastle	2,940	2,949	1,963
Nottingham	682	510	330
Salford	2,181	1,769	1,094

Further good news included the award of the Victoria Cross to Private John Cunningham, a Hull man, for bravery on 13 November. There was less TB, there having been only twenty-nine cases in two months with one death, a hopeless case. When most prices were increasing, the Food Controller, Lord Devonport, announced that after 19 February potatoes could not be sold at more than 1½d per lb.

This last was cold comfort to what followed from Lord Devonport. If voluntary rationing failed, compulsion would be necessary. 'After consideration of the available stock and probable future supplies of the three most important staple foods the situation demands that the following must be regarded as a maximum scale of allowances' for one person per week: bread 4 lb, meat 2½lb and sugar 1lb. Meat was to be consumed once a day. A household of four adopting this voluntary scale would have eight loaves, 10lb of meat and 3lb of sugar between them a week.

Following the voluntary restrictions was straightforward, and many goods were unrestricted to be freely purchased. The total amount of raw meat (and bone), bacon, poultry, rabbits and game should not exceed 2½lb. Bread, cakes and biscuits should not exceed 4lb per person per week. If flour was used, for every 1½lb, a 2lb loaf had to be given up. The ¾lb of sugar a week was for all purposes. Unrestricted substitutes for meat included fish, eggs, bones for soup, cheese, suet, lentils, peas and beans. Alternatives to wheat included oatmeal, barley meal, potatoes, rice, sago and tapioca. Lord Derby told the country to

The Hull PoW Committee shop for relatives where they could buy goods that the Red Cross would then send on to Germany.

'Stick it out – whatever the cost, whatever the privation, stick it out to the bitter end.'

Later in the year, residents were urged to sign a food economy pledge. When they sent it to the National War Savings Committee they would be enrolled, receive a pledge card and be entitled to wear the Voluntary Rations badge of a purple ribbon.

Even today with health and safety measures, railways are dangerous places. They were more so then. In the space of a few days two people were accidentally killed by trains. At Springhead, the mutilated and decapitated body of Charles Soofman, a moulder who lived at 51 Plane Street, was found. He had been hit by a train on his way to work. In Beverley, Richard Hewitt, a retired shipping agent and rope and twine dealer, aged seventy, was struck and killed by a locomotive when he was crossing the line at the station. It emerged at the inquest he was very deaf.

In February, magistrates had a difficult decision to take with regard to a bright four-year-old boy whose mother was in prison. Her crime was keeping him with her in a house in Tomlinson Street used for immoral purposes. He was so small he had to be placed on a desk so the magistrates could see him. The decision was whether to send him to a remand home – he had done nothing wrong – to Barnado's or to a neighbour who was happy to look after him while the father, who was in France, made a decision. As this would take time it was decided to place him in a Remand Home and make sure he had no contact with the other boys. A kinder decision was made in regard to George Reed. His child had died, so before starting his two month sentence for stealing eggs and stores from a ship at Victoria Dock, he was granted bail so he could attend the funeral.

Predicted shortages became actual shortages: manpower and paper. The War Office suddenly cancelled all exemptions for men aged eighteen to twenty-two who had been passed for general service and ordered the immediate call-up, including from government establishments like Customs & Excise, Post Office and local government men such as teachers. There was a ray of light for some of the men in Hull; it did not apply to these engaged in agriculture, steel production, mines, quarries, railway shops, transport work, shipyards or men covered by the Trade Cards scheme. Also called up were men in groups B2 and C2 if not in exempted categories above.

With increasing demand for artillery shells, production was increased. A further 30,000 workers were wanted for the shell-filling factories. A shortage of working class women meant that women of a higher class were needed but the work was thrown open to anyone. Pay rates were high and there was so much interest that application forms soon ran out.

There was not as much interest in sponsoring a local PoW. The Fund for Local Units needed a further 200 people to adopt a soldier or sailor in Germany. Only 157 had been adopted so far. The reason was probably cost. To provide each man with three 10lb parcels of food and 13lb of bread every fortnight cost £2 every four weeks.

The paper shortage hit the newspapers at the start of the year with a decrease of fifty per cent and threats of further reductions. This was to increase space for food and munitions imports. Newsprint was now £28 compared to its pre-war cost of £9 6s 8d a ton. Both the *Hull Daily Mail* and *Hull Times* were able to absorb the extra cost for some time by increasing advertisement rates. Inevitably both went up in price, the *Hull Daily Mail* to 1d from 12 March and the *Hull Times* to 1½d from 17 March. At the same time, both papers were purchasing and collecting waste paper for recycling – books, ledgers and pamphlets were sought, in any quantity.

IN HONOUR BOUND
WE ADOPT
THE NATIONAL SCALE
OF
VOLUNTARY RATIONS

M.F. 9.

With unrestricted submarine warfare there was a real need to reduce food consumption. The first attempt in 1917 was voluntary and was not the great success the government hoped. Further food shortages meant that compulsory rationing would need to be introduced. A placard to put in the window of households that followed the voluntary restrictions.

Looking at the following stories from a twenty-first century perspective it is difficult to see how they could all be reported together in such a matter-of-fact way; two murders and a notice from the Food Controller that bread could only be sold by weight.

In the same week two crimes startled Holderness, the alleged murder of an illegitimate child and a murder in broad daylight of a thirteen-year-old girl. The first case was convoluted and complicated, the second more clear-cut.

Mrs Caroline Sissons was in custody for the death of eight-month-old Nellie Sissons Greenwood, who had been found buried in the garden. Mrs Sissons claimed the death was a result of having accidentally given the baby a bottle containing a small quantity of laudanum. She had no reason to kill the baby because a family had paid her £5 for it. The coroner's evidence, which clearly pointed to strangulation, contradicted her evidence. The original cause of death was contrary to both, death by exhaustion from diarrhoea. A further autopsy showed no trace of poison in the baby's stomach. After a long and complex case at the assizes, the jury found her guilty of manslaughter and sentenced her to ten years' penal servitude. The judge however, was of the opinion that she should have been hanged.

Lily Tindale went to collect firewood at Constitution Hill but did not return. She was later found in the stack yard covered with straw. She had been violently assaulted and her throat cut so deeply that her head had nearly been severed. No weapon was found and like the above case, this one was also adjourned.

At the next hearing it was decided, even though the evidence was circumstantial, to send John William Thompson for trial at York Assizes charged with the murder of Lily. His razor had been found in a field some distance from the crime scene where he claimed to have put it in the hedgerow after cutting a sheep. The blood on his clothing though was human, and the police had been able to follow his boot prints from the farm to where the knife was found in part of a case, the other part of which was found under Lily's body. The razor was identified as his property and was normally kept on his mantelpiece. The prosecution said that he took it from the mantelpiece with the intention of killing Lily Tindale. Before his execution on 27 March 1917, he confessed to her murder.

Unlike many others places, the fact that beer prices were going up, less beer would be produced and that, only in two not very strong strengths, passed through the news quietly. Even the suggested price rise to 5d failed to generate much interest in Hull. More columns in the papers were dedicated to other drinks. Leaf tea had become scarcer due to a shortage of shipping space. On 1 January there were 130 billion lb of India, Ceylon, Java and China tea in the country, more than on 1 January 1914 (117 billion), but less than 1 January 1915 (148 billion). However, import restrictions meant a 2d per lb price rise for Ceylon tea, higher prices for bananas and that coffee and cocoa became difficult to get hold of. It is surprising then that, when tea became scarce later in the year, International Stores, a large grocery chain, suggested the answer was to drink coffee.

A manager of a Hull provision merchant told readers of the *Hull Times* that 'there was loads of stuff in the country, and the retailers generally [had] got very good stocks.' There would only be a problem if people lost their heads and ordered four times their usual quantities. His company had decided with other firms that they would only sell a customer their normal quantity. There inevitably would be price

*A sixteen-year-old Smith & Nephew
employee on a day off; the writer's
maternal grandmother, Blanche Chapman.
She could recall each of the raids on Hull,
but living on the Boulevard, was never
affected by them.*

*By late 1917 there were four services
women could work in. Hammond's
department store ran an exhibition of
women's war work to help boost
enrolment.*

increases but if there was no panic they would be gradual. One
customer he quoted normally bought 2lb of tea but had wanted 14lb.
As staff knew their customers, she was sold 2lb, as it was unpatriotic
of her to try to secure more.

In an age when there were far fewer phones, the newspaper was a
useful medium for making contact. Hull had two fever hospitals to
isolate patients with contagious feverish diseases, Hedon Road and
Sutton. Each week the progress of the patients was reported in the *Hull
Times*. Anonymity was maintained by each patient being issued a
number which relatives knew. Can we today imagine what it must have
felt like to read these reports? A typical example is shown below – end

of February and two weeks later. Deaths do not appear to have been reported.

> Week ending 24 February:
> Dangerously ill: 131; Very poorly: 118, 133, 134, 138, 144, 145 and 150; Slightly better: 135 and 136; Poorly but no cause for anxiety: 129, 132, 137, 139, 140, 141, 142, 143, 146, 147, 148, 151, 152 and 153; progressing satisfactorily: 96, 99, 109, 110, 117, 119, 120, 126, 127 and 130; Not so well: 85 and 112; Convalescent: all others

> Week ending 10 March:
> Progressing satisfactorily: 85, 109, 117, 119, 138, 140, 143, 146, 147 and 153; Very poorly: 140; Not as well as yesterday: 148; Slightly better: 118, 133 and 134; Not so well: 112; Poorly no concern: 129 and 148; Clothes required for 133 and 146.

Not all deaths recorded in the Roll of Honour were caused by enemy action. Like people at home, many died in accidents or from illness. Such losses were no less devastating. One such loss in February was Private William Stephenson, who died on active service of pneumonia. 'The dearly beloved and eldest son of Mr and Mrs Stephenson of 69, Alliance Avenue, aged thirty-five. From his sorrowing father, mother and family.'

Whilst the majority of the deaths and casualties were borne by average families, Hull also lost the sons of the well-known and men well-known in their own field. The Chairman of Hull Association Football Club and his wife, James and Kate Ellen Spring of 401 Anlaby Road, lost their son, Lance Corporal George Lewis, a Hull Pal serving with 10th East Yorkshires, in the fighting at Oppy Wood. He had served in Egypt and France and had refused a commission. Harry Wallace, Hull half-back, was killed on 8 May by a shell that burst near him, killing Howell Rees as well, another prominent football player.

A serious food shortage now became apparent. From the end of March only the new war loaf could be sold and there were restrictions on how old it had to be before it could be sold. No more fresh bread! The citizens of Hull were no doubt pleased that it was better than German war bread which was made from rye, potatoes and wheat, but it was not as popular as 100 per cent wheat bread although it was more filling. It was dark and had a lower food value being made of wheat, with any of the following added to make up the weight: rice, barley, maize, semolina, oats, rye or beans. This was followed by a 1d increase in price. A 4lb loaf now cost 1 shilling.

Coupled with the real shortage of flour came a warning that there might not be potatoes in May and June and that there were anxieties about the sugar supply. Naturally this led to profiteering, with nearly 300 cases a day of retailers selling at excess prices. Anyone who found a tradesman charging more than they had done the previous Friday was asked to report it to the Ministry of Food.

A few days later, the Food Controller indicated that, unless the new restrictions worked, there would a need for rationing by ticket. He urged the public to eat less bread and not waste it. If everyone ate 1lb less a week, he announced to the country that they could laugh at the submarines.

This was followed after Easter by regulations that would destroy afternoon tea at Hull's best hotels. 'No person shall after 21st April make or attempt to make for sale or after the 24th have in his possession for sale any crumpet, muffin, teacake or fancy bread or any light or fancy pastries, or any like article.' Cakes, buns, scones and biscuits which were permitted could only have a fixed amount of flour and sugar.' Cake could consist of no more than thirty per cent wheaten flour and fifteen per cent sugar, a bun fifty and ten, while a biscuit could contain no more than fifteen per cent sugar, the remainder flour. Ornamental cakes were prohibited and nothing could be added to a cake before or during baking. Teashops would now be rationed in breadstuffs and cakes, and between 3 and 6pm a customer was similarly rationed to no more than 2oz in all of bread and cake.

Meat again became an issue. If all grain was for human consumption then there would be a shortage of animal feed and surplus cattle would have to be slaughtered. Not even turnips were available to feed the cattle – they were too expensive. Coupled with only a little reduction in meat consumption, this led to a leading city butcher predicting a shortage before mid-June. That there would be a shortage was certain. He advocated two meatless days a week.

With such shortages it is highly unlikely anyone in Hull cared about the report in the papers that Denmark was down to three weeks' supply of margarine. But when they found out that there was no margarine on the market in London either, almost certainly their attitude changed. A wholesale buyer told them that margarine was 'not to be bought for love or money.' However, there was plenty of butter, if you could afford it, but not enough to last as a substitute for everyone. Again this was blamed on import restrictions and further shortages were likely. When the butter ran short 'for those with money there were vegetable replacements' such as nut butter.

A sugar shortage had been mentioned earlier in the year. A sure sign that is was in short supply was apparent after 1 June when sugar content in sweets was reduced from fifty to twenty-five per cent. Fortunately there was still sufficient so that there was no change in jam, marmalade and condensed milk.

In some cases it was not a shortage of food that caused the difficulties but one of labour. Food was being wasted because there was no one to deal with the imports. Perishable foodstuffs were found lying around the docks in boxes in the summer heat. Tons of bacon went to grease and soap manufacturers because it was no longer edible, while in other towns there was a serious shortage. The figures show the level of wastage. During the year 772,894 lb of beef, eggs, fruit and vegetables were condemned and 1,130 bags of onions destroyed as unsound. One Hull wag wrote about the waste: 'Many towns can hardly get bacon or ham at all. But let them cheer up, we will send it to them from Hull in the derivative form of soap and grease.' This was not only a problem for Hull. There were tons of food on London docks waiting to be moved but there was insufficient labour, and, in many cases, no-one knew who it belonged to or where it was to be sent.

As Hull was also a fishing port the government might have expected cheap herrings to appeal there, but it was not popular. It was noted that the herrings had been put 'on the market in Hull with disastrous results.' So poor was their reception that the writer thought that they would not even be able to give them away, they were just too salty. The only positive thing that could be said was that the herrings had been bought to stop the Germans eating them, but would the Germans have done so?

Even if more land was cultivated there would still be food shortages. One idea was to reduce waste by recycling food for pigs; another was to kill vermin, animals that consumed or spoiled human food. Reducing the number of pests would cut food loss. The Food Production Department urged farmers to reduce the number of rookeries and urged tenants to destroy rabbits by shooting and trapping. They suggested forming rat and sparrow clubs, hiring professional rat catchers and rewarding other persons at rates which should not exceed 1s per dozen

Residents of Constable Street pose in front of their Roll of Honour.

rats' tails; 3d per dozen heads of fully fledged house sparrows; 2d per dozen of unfledged house sparrows; 1d per dozen house sparrows eggs. There was no money from the government, it was to come from interested parties and voluntary sources, but some might come from district and parish councils if they felt it appropriate. A year later, rat damage to food was estimated to be £40 million.

The call-ups and attempts to be exempted continued but at least in the army the men would be guaranteed food. Three cases from March are representative of the year. James Starkey, an entertainer, was charged with failing to join the army. He had been found at his mother's house, 13, Brighton Terrace, and taken to Central Police Station. He was happy to join and had tried to join 7 Duke of Wellington's Regiment (DWR) but had been rejected; neither had he been called up. No fine was imposed and he was handed over to the military. Another case was that of an unnamed grocer with a bad speech impediment and distressing domestic situation as one of his children was deaf and dumb. A Salvation Army officer wrote to the tribunal that his call-up would inflict great hardship on his family. His exemption was renewed. A medical grade C2, twenty-nine-year-old coal merchant of thirteen years, who worked alone with one horse and rulley, was also given further extension. The randomness of the tribunal's decision is clear. No comment was made about the physicality of his work even though he told them he had heart trouble and muscular rheumatism. A case elsewhere had resulted in the man being drafted and told that the army would cure him!

Not every male from Hull wanted to stay out of the army. Most went when called-up. Although not called up, James Houston, a future Hull doctor, made a very long journey to enlist. In 1914 he was staying with a French family in an area that was overrun by the Germans. He avoided internment through the kindness of his hosts and the excellence of his French. When he reached the age for military service he walked home through Switzerland and joined the Tank Corps.

Around the same time, someone who did not wish to serve in the military, Richard Evans, a Quaker who would be a founder of Adult Education in Hull, was on the Western Front. Although working as a stretcher bearer, he was recalled to serve eighteen months in Wakefield gaol because he had not registered for military service.

Any news about a Hull soldier, even if they had emigrated six years before the war, was worth printing; someone would know him. There was one special story in the papers in mid-April. Lieutenant Walter Partis, serving in the Australian Light Horse, captured a German Prince. In March, while on patrol in No-Man's Land they came across Prince Frederic Karl of Prussia trying to get back to his lines after being shot down. He was shot trying to escape from the Australians but taken back to their lines and sent to hospital, where he died.

At Arras, the British Army was making final preparations for the assault on Vimy Ridge. In Hull it was Easter and two local Volunteer Battalions were going to Camp. Good Friday was spent quietly with many people indulging in a country ramble. Even though there was snow on the ground 'the sun shone with summer-like brilliance.' Despite the snow, many worked on their allotments. In the afternoon, a crowd of over 6,000 watched Hull beat rivals Rovers at the Boulevard. Cinemas were well patronised but, as was usual, there was no music allowed. At the City Art Gallery, for the admission price of 7d, including tax, a display of Canadian war photographs could be seen. The paper warned potential visitors that the photos 'of German dead lying lifeless...[were]...particularly repulsive.'

Charity collection on a large scale has been mentioned a number of times. There were also smaller charities and groups collected to help in whatever way they could. Typical examples were the girls of Chapman Street School. On Wednesday, 4 April at 3.45 pm with the help of girls from other schools, they staged an entertainment show. 'At the end of the numerous performances visitors contributed £1 5s.'

Even before the verdicts on the previous murder cases had been decided, there were two further murders, this time both in Hull. Private Fred Dry, a teacher, serving with the East Yorkshire Regiment, was charged with the murder of his thirty-two-year-old wife Madge at their home, 12 Marne Street, while on sick leave from the Northern General Hospital in Leicester. The second murder involved two Norwegian sailors; eighteen-year-old Boye Andersen was charged with the murder of John Johnson. He was accused of stabbing the second officer of the Hull steamer *Fredhelm* in the chest.

Madge Dry's death was brutal. She was found in the bedroom with thirteen puncture wounds in her body; six were over the heart and four in the neck. In a chair near her body was a bayonet stained with blood, nine inches along the blade, and elsewhere in the house an eighteen inch long, one-and-a-half inch wide iron bar was found. The autopsy revealed that her lung had been penetrated and her heart twice. Her skull was fractured and her brain lacerated. The verdict was simple, wilful murder against same, by person unknown.

At his trial it was pointed that Private Dry had found her and gone to the police to report her death. There was no blood on his clothing and there were no witnesses. He was discharged but later re-arrested and sent for trial at York Assizes. The jury couldn't agree a verdict so the judge adjourned the case to the next assizes.

At the same time there was a fatal quarrel in Alfred Gelder Street. This was clearer cut. A conversation had turned to an argument with the deceased hitting the defendant twice before he retaliated. With the story being corroborated by witnesses, William Tulley was released and Anthony McGowan's demise was recorded as death by misadventure; he had struck his head on the pavement when he fell during the fight.

Murder, accidental death and then a double love suicide. A young Hull couple ended their lives simply because they could not bear to be parted. David McDonald, of 4 Mason Street, a joiner's apprentice, had three brothers serving and a fourth who had been killed. He was in love with sixteen-year-old Doris Hudson of 14 Rose Terrace, a brush maker, who reciprocated his feelings.

When he was called up they decided to never be separated. On 7 May he wrote to his mother from Beverley. 'Dear Mother, I am sorry to tell you that Doris and I have decided to go away, as we cannot bear the thought of parting from one another through my having to join the army. We don't see why we should endure misery…and we don't see why I should go to the war and perhaps be killed…Thank Mary and Jack for their kindness to Doris and myself, give the rest of my brothers and sisters my best love, and I thank you dear mother, from the bottom of my heart, for all you have done for me. Good-bye for the present. – I remain your loving son. Dave.' Doris left home at 6.15 am the same day, saying she was seeing her sweetheart off at the station. Ninety minutes later her mother found a note in the sitting room saying that she would never see her again and asking her forgiveness. After a search they were found in Beverley Beck tied together by a boot string. On David's body was a notebook containing messages to members of his family. Again, it was plain that death was a constant part of life and the news.

And then there was sex. Seventeen-year-old Mary Ford was charged at Hull with nine indictments for procuring, pleading guilty on two counts. She occupied premises on which she allowed young girls to be present for immoral purposes. As she was a minor, she was given three years in Borstal.

By 1917 Hull and New Holland had real guns. When these were fired in practice, as on 16 and 17 May between 10 am and 4.30 pm, this was noted in the papers. Possibly this was a response to the fiasco with a wooden gun and to show residents they would now be protected, or the purpose may have been to stop a possible panic caused by people mistakenly thinking there was a raid.

Whether they felt safe after reading in the local papers about the London raid of 13 June is uncertain, especially as London had a considerable number of guns to defend it. Wednesday, 13 June was a sunny day and no one was expecting 14 Gothas to appear above London. This was the first daylight raid on London It caused 162 deaths and 432 injuries and was the deadliest raid of the war. 'Keeping out of range of anti-aircraft fire, they dropped high-explosive bombs from East Ham westwards to Holborn, and from Bermondsey northwards to Stamford Hill. Eighteen children were killed when a bomb penetrated the roof of a London County Council school in Poplar, and exploded in the infants' department killing every pupil, although their teacher survived. Railway termini were targeted: 16 were killed by the bomb at Liverpool Street, and 19 at Fenchurch Street. The whole glass frontage of the nearby Albion Clothing Store was blown out. A bus conductor lay on the pavement with her leg severed at the knee by a shard of glass. A No 25 bus stood by the kerb containing a solitary passenger sitting behind the driver's seat: he was hunched forward, killed by a piece of glass that had pierced his neck.' No Gotha was lost.

Probably in response to this air raid, instructions were issued for Hull. 'In the event of a hostile air raid over Hull in the daytime, all buzzers will sound for five minutes and the public are earnestly requested to seek shelter until the buzzers sound again for five minutes which will signify that all is clear.'

A young Hull man who was unlikely to be called to the colours. In his lapel he is wearing a numbered badge that shows he is on important civilian war work.

By 1917 even the YMCA had adopted military attire for its staff.

After a night raid on 22 August in southern England and an attack on nearby Hedon during the night of 21 August, the *Hull Times* published a poem. Entitled *Prayer for a Raid Night*, penned by Lillian Hume of Westbourne Avenue, it surely summed up what most thought when the buzzers went.

'O Saviour of the world! In Thy great might,
Be with us thro' this wakeful, watchful night;
Protect our airmen in flights perilous,
So fearless risking life and limb for us;
Give little children sleep, give sick folk peace,
That pain and dread, and restlessness may cease;
Of Thy great love soothe out, with tender touch,
All pangs of fright from hearts which fear too much;
What if swift death should to Thy people come –
Would it not only be a quick call home?
Of Thine aid certain – of Thy promise sure,
We rest within Thy love, serene, secure.'

A letter from a builder in Hitching published in the *Hull Times* may have allayed some readers' fears. 'The safest place in raids is under the stairs. They are constructed so that the greater the weight thrown on them the firmer they become.'

Hull had been lucky again. 'On the night of 21 August 1917 a contentious Zeppelin raid took place over the East Riding and Hull. Officially denied by British authorities at the time, it is now clear that at least three out of a fleet of eight Zeppelins made landfall in the area and dropped their bombs. *L41* (Hauptmann Manger) was driven off by gunfire from Hull, instead dropping his bombs on Paull, Preston, Thorngumbald and Hedon. Only Hedon suffered damage, which included the destruction of a Methodist chapel and damage to other properties. One man was injured.'

By 1917 the St John's Ambulance Brigade no longer wore the type of uniform seen in the 1914 photograph. Khaki was the colour of service.

On 24/25 September, *L41* returned again, dropped sixteen bombs and, fortunately for Hull, only injured three people. Dora Willatt wrote to her sweetheart in France the next day. 'We had a Zepp raid last night...The buzzers went at 11 pm. Ma made me get up and we all dozed downstairs and a bomb woke us up at 2.45 am – there were one or two explosions but the searchlights never caught it. They were on until 5 and the relief went at 5.30 but we got rather fed up and went to bed at 4. They have been very near the Naval Hospital and an aerial torpedo went into its garden and broke some windows and the Matron and the Fleet Surgeon nearly got a brick against their heads.'

Again Hull was lucky. On 20 October, *L41* and *L45* made landfall near the Humber. After circling around Withernsea for about an hour, they moved towards the Midlands. *L55*, under the same orders to attack northern industrial cities, claimed to have dropped 4,400 lbs of bombs on Mappleton and Hull before attacking what they believed was Sheffield or Birmingham. They had bombed Holme near Peterborough and scattered sixteen bombs between Hitchin and Hatfield.

How well was the war going? Many Hull residents might have wondered this after reading about the raid, one in a string of German air raids, and then at the same time about the recent shipping losses. In the week ending 10 June, thirty ships were lost (of which twenty-one were large), eighteen ships having been lost the week before, as well as six trawlers compared with five in the previous week. These were acknowledged to be the highest losses for both in a month.

Was there any good news? Some. The British Oil and Cake Mill Company was doing well, showing profits of £293,826 after tax. For those lucky enough to have shares, this gave a dividend of fifteen per cent. Then there was the amazing story of Private Samuel Blackshaw, of 6 Lockwood Terrace, who had worked for Messrs G. Brown, shipbuilders, before the war. He had volunteered on 7 September 1914 and gone to France in April 1915, where he was made a PoW. After being sent to four camps, he eventually escaped and arrived home in Hull on 31 May. A second VC had been won by a Hull-born resident – this time by an officer and international rugby player, Second Lieutenant John 'Jack' Harrison, for bravery on 3 May at Oppy Wood. Beer drinkers welcomed the government's change of heart in allowing an increase in production of thirty-three per cent. Increasing the amount of light beer and decreasing heavy beer production would give a fifty per cent increase.

During such troubled times a royal visit was always welcome news. In the middle of June, the King and Queen began a tour of the industrial north-east coast, finishing with a visit to the Humber district on 18 June. Lord Nunburnholme was in overall charge of the arrangements.

Just in case the loyal population of Hull needed reminding about an appropriate patriotic welcome, the Mayor wrote in the *Hull Times* to remind them. 'We are to be honoured by a gracious visit from their Majesties the King and Queen on Monday next, the 18th inst., and I shall be most glad if the citizens, so far as they can, will display flags as an appropriate indication of their gratification for the honour conferred upon the city by Their Majesties' proposed visit.'

Needless to say his wish was respected and the visit was a great success. The Royal Party arrived at Paragon Station in sunshine, to flags and bunting displayed across the town. They were received by Lord Nunburnholme and wife, the Lord and Lady Mayoress, the High Steward and other dignitaries. Their first visit was Earle's shipyard followed by refreshments and then they went to C.D. Holmes' engineering works to inspect the erecting shop for minesweepers' engines. After a short visit to the Guildhall and a nearly two-hour lunch, during which they unexpectedly visited the rest station on Paragon Station, they inspected the Voluntary Aid Detachment (VAD) hospital on Cottingham Road and the Royal Navy hospital on Argyle Street. For the thousands gathered in the Hull City ground, the investiture was the highlight. The King presented medals to 173 officers, NCOs and men. They left Hull promptly at 4.30 p.m. After the visit the King wrote to the mayor. 'The warm and loyal welcome from your city was indeed a happy conclusion to a most interesting visit to the North-East counties.'

 A few days later, Lord Nunburnholme shared a letter with the citizens of Hull. 'Dear Lord Nunburnholme, the King and Queen desire me to let you know how much pleased they were to be able to visit your county and see for themselves the important war work which is being carried out in Hull…it was gratifying to the King and Queen to be able to include the two hospitals in the programme. His Majesty did not fail to notice the fine appearance of the East Yorkshire Volunteer Force as he passed between their ranks. All the arrangements were well planned and carried out, and the King and Queen returned to London with a pleasing impression of their welcome in Hull.'

As if the visit wasn't enough in itself, during his visit to the north, the King had been told that beer was both dear and scarce. As a result of this, prices went down from 16 July.

To help combat poor-quality child care, many cities and towns participated in the National Baby Week held from 1 to 7 July. The week's aim was to highlight ways to reduce the high rate of infant mortality. It pulled no punches with its statements: 'every minute a baby dies in the UK; in 1915, nine soldiers and twelve babies died every hour; in 1915, 89,477 children under 1 died in England and Wales; out of every 1,000 babies born, eleven die during the first twenty-four hours, twenty-two during the first week and thirty-six in the first month; out of every 1,000 babies born, 250 die at birth or in the first year.' The causes were simple to identify, the remedies more difficult to apply: bad housing; improper feeding; maternal ignorance; and the difficulty in obtaining pure milk.

Although a hardworking and pro-active city in many respects during the war, Hull was backward in its observance of National Baby Week and in crèche provision. In other towns, that had followed London's lead, there had been lectures on child care and health and baby parades. Hull's contribution had been a Flag Day, selling flags with the words 'Save the babies' and on the reverse 'Help the Hull day crèches'.

The third anniversary of the outbreak of war was impressively observed in Hull. The Archbishop of Hull preached in Holy Trinity to a crowded congregation and afterwards the Lord

WHEN THE RAIDERS CAME

were you and your family insured?

If you are not already "covered" take advantage of the

£25,000 FREE AIR RAID AND **BOMBARDMENT INSURANCE**

Offered by the

ILLUSTRATED

SUNDAY HERALD

Order a copy To-day.

THREE-HALFPENCE.

Readers of the Sunday Herald could get £25,000 of air raid insurance. After the raids began, it is safe to assume that a number of Hull residents took advantage of the offer.

Mayor held a public meeting in Guildhall Square. There was no formal procession because it was Market Day. A resolution was submitted and carried 'that on this the third anniversary of the declaration of a righteous war, this meeting of the citizens of Hull records its inflexible determination to continue to a victorious end the struggle in maintenance of those ideals of liberty and justice which are the common and sacred cause of the Allies.' *O God, Our help In Ages Past* was sung and the proceedings closed with the National Anthem.

The citizens of Hull displayed a lack of patriotism on August Bank holiday when large queues formed to buy tickets at Paragon to widespread destinations. There were no excursions, so few travelled long distances. Although such travel was officially discouraged, large numbers went to the Yorkshire coastal towns regardless. The cabbies were very busy and newspaper boys changed their professions and became porters as there were so few of these due to the draft. This was countered by the patriotism of others and there were Flag Day sellers everywhere.

Mention has been made of brave Hull men. In August there was a story about a brave young Hull woman. Ada Jackson, a Girl Guide, was swimming in the sea at Withernsea when she noticed munition worker, Lucy Tindall, of 44 Clarendon Street, in difficulty. As she was going down for the third time, Ada managed to catch her round the chest and pull her out. After half an hour on the sands, Lucy was better.

This was followed by a further civilian bravery story, this time of a workman who risked his life. Four-year-old George Tether, of 2 Sutton Grove, was playing near a brick pond at Stoneferry when he fell in. His mother, up to her waist in the pond, cried for help as she was trying to rescue him. Repairing the road nearby, James Robinson, of 40 Estcourt Street, heard the shouting and rushed over. Seeing the problem, he quickly took off his jacket and waistcoat and jumped in. As the boy's head was sinking he grabbed his hair and dragged him ashore, where he was found to be no worse for wear.

At last something was being done about meat prices. Eventually something would be done about availability as well. In September, the Food Controller issued an order fixing wholesale maximum dead meat prices and regulated the retail price to the consumer. Further good news was that butter imports had restarted.

	Beef & Veal			Mutton & Lamb		Pork	
	Price per stone			Price per stone		Price per stone	
	Home killed	Imported		Home killed	Imported	Home killed	Imported
	Carcase	Hind qtrs.	Fore qtrs.	Carcase	Carcase	Carcase	Carcase
1917	s d	s d	s d	s d	s d	s d	s d
Sept.	8 8	8 4	7 0	8 8	7 8	9 6	8 6
Oct.	8 4	8 0	6 8	8 8	7 8	9 6	8 6
Nov.	8 0	7 8	6 4	8 8	7 8	9 6	8 6
Dec	8 0	7 8	6 4	8 8	7 8	9 6	8 6
1918							
Jan.	7 4	7 0	5 8	8 8	7 8	9 6	8 6

This was followed by the Bacon, Ham, and Lard (Maximum Prices) Order, 1917 that set the maximum price that could be charged to retailers by importers, curers and manufacturers. Lord Yapp also gave advice. 'Wherever possible, save bread by eating potatoes. Economise all round. Conserve tinned and preserved fruits, using instead available fresh-grown supplies. Apples and pears should be dried for use when fruit will be very scarce.'

It was all well and good having meat to cook if there were no matches to light the cooker. One local resident suggested that it was easy to overcome the match shortage. However, the answer needed at least one match to make it work. Buy an old-fashioned penny lamp, and keep it on night and day. The pint of paraffin it needed, the writer said, would last a long time.

The Darby family of 32 Lorraine Street probably wished they had been unable to buy matches when two-year-old Thomas died of burns. The mother got up to light the fire, leaving him and his five-year-old sister in bed in the front bedroom. She heard screams and returned to find him on fire. She quickly wrapped him to extinguish the flames and took him to the infirmary. After asking for a drink, he lapsed into unconsciousness and died. Mrs Darby found matches on the floor. It transpired that he had the matches and in a struggle with his sister, who was trying to take them away, they somehow ignited and his flannelette nightshirt caught fire. The inquest verdict was straightforward; accidental death due to shock.

The dedication of a rather large street shrine somewhere in Hull.

The home Lieutenant Harrison VC left when he went to war, 75 Wharncliffe Avenue.

Then there was the weather and its effect on supplies. 'After one of the most miserable Augusts on record, September opened even worse in the Hull district, ranging from a mere drizzle to a regular soaking. Harvest prospects grow more and more dim.'

In September two novel ways of staying out of the army were noted. These were killing yourself or trying to, and cross-dressing. John Coward, a soldier home on leave, went into the backyard of his home, 6 Ellen Grove. A few minutes later he was heard to shout 'Emily!'. His wife rushed out to find him cutting his throat. She called an officer who took him to the infirmary. He survived the war. Another, reported in the *Hull Times*, concerned Alfred Dunn, aged forty, and Lillian Fletcher, aged forty-five. Whether they were locals is not mentioned but they were remanded in Bristol for failing to produce their registration cards. When a detective called he was told the only other person in the house was Lillian's sister, who was too ill to be seen. The detective went to the room and found Dunn in women's clothes. He said he was her sister but the detective was suspicious and pulled his hair, which proved to be a wig. He then admitted wearing women's clothes to avoid military service as he was a conscientious objector.

Lord Nunburnholme, Lord Lieutenant of the East Riding in his role as Commanding Offficer of the Volunteers.

In June the King and Queen visited the north-east to see the important work being done there. The last stop was Hull, which greatly impressed them.

Not everyone wanted to stay out of the war. On 1 September, the Admiralty announced the capture in the North Sea of a small boat containing six German prisoners. The boat was spotted 170 miles from land by a trawler that informed a destroyer, which recaptured them. They were submariners, some of whom had been awarded the Iron Cross. On capture they expressed their frustration saying that they would have reached Germany in twenty-four hours. The coble they had stolen was from Scarborough.

Three days later, at 6.50 pm, Scarborough was under shellfire. A thick mist hung over the sea when one or possibly more subs fired into the town. Minesweepers in South Bay fired at a sub in North Bay. Two people were killed, Thomas Pickup and Mrs Elizabeth Scott. They both died at their homes on Northside. The firing lasted ten minutes and caused considerable damage. There was no panic. The submarine(s) disappeared before the destroyers arrived.

At the quarter session in Scarborough a Hull soldier, twenty-nine-year-old Thomas Watson, was sentenced to three years' penal servitude. His crime was breaking into shops and stealing jewellery valued at £524 19s 6d. All the property was recovered after a roof-top chase.

There had been requests for footballs and other sporting equipment, for books to pass the time and spare clothing. Just before Christmas, Private Cooke asked the Hull public for seven or eight complete Pierrot costumes and any music that could be spared. This was to allow him and five other Hull lads to make the spare time of the lads in his company merrier.

Neither petty crime nor drunkenness went away. Each week the court heard cases so similar to those heard previously there is nothing to be gained from recording them, apart from the cases of two Lascar seamen and three soldiers. Both of the seamen were charged with being drunk and disorderly, but one was also sentenced for assaulting an officer, kicking, biting and hitting him on the cheek. One of the soldiers, Private J. Kavanagh, charged with being an absentee, had no idea where his uniform was. Another appeared for the same reason in his full kit with pack and helmet, ready to go back to the front. The third soldier beat them both. Twenty-year-old Private Frederick Erwin Walker was charged with being absent for the sixth time. As he had three gold wound stripes, he was told to do his duty, though obviously he had already been doing that. All three were handed over to escorts.

Some crimes were more heinous than others, some so heinous that they were never fully reported. In late September, at Hull Police Court, Geoffrey Pickering, a twenty-five-year-old solicitor, and Laurence Clarence, a thirty-five-year-old officer in the Australian Army, were committed to the York Assizes. The offences were alleged to have been committed on various dates between March and August. Clarence was given bail on a surety of £1,000. No further reports were carried by the papers. It is reasonable to presume that the criminal status of homosexual acts at that time, and the taboo surrounding the subject generally, may explain this.

This was also probably the case with another unspecified offence. A 'serious charge was preferred against Haakim Benson, twenty-five, a Swede, and a boy.' The boy was caught after a chase. Both were remanded and nothing further was printed about the story.

There were moments of fun. People still met to play games in their spare time, sometimes seriously. Whist was one such game. In the Hull and District Whist Association, Albert Recreation and Albert Somerset merged to quickly become the dominant team. Then there was the Druids Domino League, bowls at Gipsyville and horse racing.

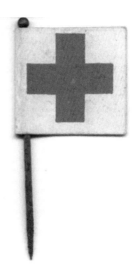

Probably the most numerous Flag Days were for the Red Cross which contributed much to the war effort.

Although a register of enemy aliens had been taken at the start of the war, it did not stop the authorities losing contact with them. George Trotter, of 36 Mayfield Street, was sentenced to six months' imprisonment for having, as an enemy alien, entered a prohibited area and resided there – South Shields. He claimed to be an Australian with British parentage and a German wife. He said he had lived in a number of countries, served in the Dutch Army and British RGA, and worked as a baker for a German firm. When his parents died at the age of seven he was living in New York. His only explanation for his foreign accent was that he had been working with a number of Germans. Evidence showed he had left Dantzic (sic) in 1889. The Magistrate commented that there was no doubt the country was honey-combed with Germans, who were collecting information to the detriment of the country.

The patriotic contribution made by one family was recorded in October. Seven sons and a son-in-law of Mrs Baldwin, a widow – her husband had been a trawler skipper – who lived at 21 Eton Street, had been or were with the colours. Her eldest son, thirty-three-year old Robert, a chief engineer on a naval trawler, was lost at sea on 18 May. His wife and four children lived at 16 Scarborough Street. Thirty-one-

year-old J.A. was also a chief engineer on a naval trawler, whose wife
and three children lived in West Dock Avenue. Her next son, J.T., had
been in France for twelve months and had also worked on trawlers
before emigrating to Canada where he had joined the army. He had a
wife and two children in Canada, as did also her fourth son, also an ex-
trawler man, who had emigrated to Canada and joined the army there.
Another son was a chief engineer on a naval trawler based in Sheerness,
where his wife lived. Private J, aged twenty-one, had worked for Smith
and Nephew before the war. He had served in the Northumberland
Fusiliers (NF) and then Machine Gun Corps (MGC) before being
invalided home from France after being buried in a shell hole. W.S.,
the youngest son, was nineteen and serving in France with the Tank
Corps where he had been for a year. He had also worked at Smith and
Nephew. The final member of the family was twenty-six-year-old son-
in-law S. Harrison, who had served in the RFA. After two years in
France, he had been wounded in the thigh and hospitalised for eighteen
weeks. Employed before the war at Jackson's furniture stores, he had
lived with his wife at 10 Belgrave Terrace.

At the end of November the Lord Mayor presented Private Robert
Galbraith, of 88 Winberg Street, who had served with the 4th East
Yorkshire Regiment, a hand-propelled chair, provided by the Lord
Kitchener National Memorial Fund, for his use as long as he needed
it. The nineteen-year-old joiner had enlisted at seventeen, volunteered
for France when he was eighteen and been injured on 5 November
1916 serving with the Border Regiment. He was wounded in the body
and hand and had both legs amputated. Shortly before this presentation
came the news that those widowed after 1 July 1916 would receive a
£5 bounty. How this must have made women widowed earlier feel was
not discussed.

Men like Galbraith helped make toys for Christmas. The Hull Lord
Roberts Home for Disabled Soldiers and Sailors ran a memorial
workshop making wooden toys at reasonable prices. They were
'skilfully fashioned and painted to amuse youngsters.'

Compensation for injury is not a new idea. Soldiers received a
pension and workers used the law to get what they could. Lily Hulturn,
an infant in the eyes of the law, that is she was under the age of
majority, claimed increased compensation from the Modern Printers
Ltd., New Cleveland Street. A serious accident resulted in amputation

of her right thumb and second finger and damage to rest of the hand in September 1916. She was given 8/4d a week but could by late 1917 have been earning 30s a week. The judge found in favour of the appellant and awarded her 7s per week compensation, on condition her employers found her suitable work for which she was to receive a further 14s per week.

Money was at the heart of the three-month-old dispute in the Hull painting trade. It was settled on Friday 7 December with normal work to be resumed on Monday. From then, men would be paid 11½d per hour, with any other issues to be dealt with later by the Yorkshire Joint Council.

Wages had risen, but prices were rising at least as fast and there were shortages of labour, materials and goods. Christmas 1917 would be miserable and one of austerity and practicality, the leader writer of the *Hull Times* wrote. 'Although war has taught us how to be economical, it does not prevent us from keeping up old-time customs, and as winter sets in we prepare with much the old spirit for a happy Yuletide. "As Christmas comes but once a year", and then, although times have changed so much and brought sorrow to so many of us, we think of Christmas gifts for those away and at home. Before the war, stores and shop windows were crowded with innumerable gifts – some useful, others merely pretty ... But each year the nature of these presents has changed considerably...they have become useful, practical, and acceptable...[A period of austerity is]...no time for the squandering of money on trumpery finery or trivialities regardless of who it is for – it must be of a suitable, useful character.'

In the same edition, Joan Lewcock recommended gloves and hosiery and suggested a visit to Thornton Varleys where they had a good range of furs and of gifts generally. One wonders if this was independent advice?

To make sure the men serving abroad had as enjoyable a Christmas as possible, the Mayor and his wife had set themselves the task of raising £3,000 for the 20,000 men estimated to be serving outside the UK. This would provide them with a little gift of a packet of sweets, a packet of tobacco and cigarettes and a Christmas card. For Christmas 1916, chocolate had been provided – not available for Christmas 1917 – a pack of soap, insect powder – a gift from a local firm – and cigarettes.

Not all the money being spent was on Christmas. Hull was in ninth position of large towns in the provinces in respect to its contribution to the National War Loan – £875,495 by 1 December. It was below Leeds but above Bradford. Leeds may have sold more War Loans, but it didn't have Jack the giant Flemish rabbit raising funds. During its pre-Christmas travels around the city, Jack had raised £191 15s for various Hull war charities.

Finance was a problem for the Hull Poor Children's Christmas Dinner Fund. 'It may be thought that during this war time, when the working people are earning in many cases much higher wages than usual and comparatively few are out of work, there ought not to be the need for this effort…but there are many needy persons…for whom the terribly increased prices of foodstuffs makes the difficulties of having very great, and this is especially the case with the children of soldiers and navy men…gifts in money will be gratefully received.'

Three days before Christmas a message appeared in the *Hull Times:* 'The Lord Mayor and Lady Mayoress desire to convey to the citizens of Hull, and those associated with them at this season, their Greeting and Good Wishes for Christmas and the New Year.

German PoWs in a range of replacement uniforms. Many worked on farms as agricultural labourers. While most were not unhappy with their lot, a number did escape. None managed to get back to Germany.

'They feel that for all the customary festivities of the season will be restrained, especially with so many under heavy burden of anxiety respecting those dear to them who are now serving or have been wounded, and the large number in our midst bereaved of loved ones in this ruthless war whom they greet respectfully in sorrow and sympathy.

'They sincerely hope that God's good blessing may rest upon our citizens this Christmastide, and upon all our Heroic Defenders on land and sea, and bring to us, with satisfaction and joy, in the New Year, the happiness of enduring peace.'

In a different vein, a Hull man serving in the trenches also wished everyone a Merry Christmas. 'I wish ya a Merry Kissimus, Ana Happy New Year, A pocket full o' money an' a barrel full o' beer. A good fat pig that'll last ya all t'year. An' please will ya gie me me Kissimus box.'

After months of quiet the case of Private Dry was once again news. Evidence given at the assizes provided grounds for clemency: his father had died in Willerby asylum; his sister was in a home for the mental deficient; his wife was unfaithful; and he had volunteered for service overseas and gone to France on 9 December 1915. Although he was sentenced to death with a recommendation to mercy, the date of his execution was set for 9am on 11 December at Armley gaol. Naturally, he petitioned against the verdict and his appeal was heard on 17 December. On New Year's Day morning, he was notified of his reprieve. He received a custodial sentence instead.

Major John Fairfax-Blakeborough OBE, MC, a North Yorkshire man serving in the RND, wrote a regular column about the doings of the Hull soldiers he met. He sent his thoughts on Christmas from the trenches somewhere in Belgium. 'In 1914 we were certain that we should be home in 1915; when '15 came we were confident that the following Christmas would see us amongst loved ones. Then came 1917, that found us more optimistic than ever that before December arrived hostilities would be ended and those of us who were left would eat our Christmas dinner at home…Well! here we are still amongst it all on the eve of the festival of peace in a world in which there is no peace and in which hatred towards men rather than goodwill reigns supreme…The angels weep and the devils laugh.'

Hull, like everywhere else in the country, was awaiting rationing in the New Year. Although most realised it was needed and necessary, it was not wanted, so one piece of news made many feel very happy. There was to be no scheme of rationing for tobacco – it would just not be as easy to get hold of. Surprisingly, no one wrote in, as they had in Reading, suggesting that mixing dried used tea leaves in with the tobacco in 50-50 ratio would be just as enjoyable.

On the last day of the year, the *Hull Daily Mail*'s thought for the day was not about victory:

'Ring out false pride in place and blood,
the civic slander, and the spite;
Ring in the love of truth and right,
Ring in the common love of good.'

CHAPTER 5

1918:
The Final Blows

A day later, the thought for the day was 'I will maintain.' Mr. John Hodge, Minister for Pensions, previously Minister for Labour, wrote about his wish for the future. 'My greatest and most fervent hope is for an early and victorious termination of the war, such a victory as will make a similar catastrophe impossible.'

The people of Hull were told who would win the war and how to go about it in one editorial. 'The war will be "won" by the nation, or group of nations, whose civilian population can endure the most heroically, and can control itself the longest.'

While Mr. Hodge had wished for a victory 'as will make a similar catastrophe impossible', that is a repeat of the war, others had different ideas. One idea mooted was the building of a Channel tunnel after the war. Good for business, certainly, but more importantly it would be easier to supply armies in a future European conflict. Fortunately it was not built; the reverse was equally true.

What did the local papers have to say on the matter of yet another year of war? The *Eastern Morning News* hoped it would be the last year of the war. 'Another year dawns amid the booming of guns and the shock of shells. The work of killing and devastation proceeds with unbated (sic) fury. Four times now has the world entered upon a New Year with little before it but the prospect of a continuance of carnage, and we look in vain for any really hopeful sign that all this bloodshed and destruction may be on the point of coming to an end …Our hope is that before 1918 has reached its close the seal will have been set upon the conflict of Right against Might.' 'Though the clouds of war are still hovering above us, and the outlook is grim of aspect, there is no reason why the salutations belonging to the season should be withheld, and we therefore beg to wish all our readers, A Happy New Year.'

When informed of the cost of the war, many in Hull must have wondered whether the country could afford to endure. During the first nine months of the financial year, the expenditure of the United Kingdom had been £2,029 million. This was £463 million more than the corresponding period in 1916. Expenditure was running at £7 million a day.

Although Hull had successfully raised large amounts of money to buy war loans, it was still not enough. The arrival of a tank on 7 January was designed to pull even more money from pockets. It succeeded with Hull Corporation investing £100,000. 'Nelson' was parked in Victoria Square with a procession and music and speeches every day during dinner hour. Hull's target was £1 million and the city's generosity was measured on a barometer that compared Hull with Stoke and Swansea.

Over the week, money poured in. Trawler owners O. & O.S. Hellyer offered to buy a tank regardless of the cost as long as it bore the name 'The City of Hull'. By the end of the week nearly £2 million, slightly less than the Mayor's personal target of £2,100,000, had been contributed with large contributions coming in on the last day: £12,500 from Goole Shipbuilding Co.; £10,000 from Cochrane and Sons, Royal Exchange Assurance, Great Northern Steam Fishing Co., Hellyer's Steam Fishing Co. (£120,000 in all); F.O. Hellyer and O.S. Hellyer (£30,000 in all) and A. Lacey and Company. An anonymous philanthropist placed a £5 bond in the tank to the credit of the East Hull Silver Band. On the last day, between 3 and 4 pm, Lord Nunburnholme gave a prize to every twelfth investor. As a further draw to possible investors, on one occasion the mayor presented a serving East Yorkshire Regiment soldier, Corporal Simmons of 20 Emily Street, with a medal. This presentation of the MM awarded for bravery on the Somme on 15 August 1916 was made on top of the tank in front of the Sheriff and General von Donop, commander of the Humber Garrison.

How did Hull compare with other major cities? The answer is that Hull did well.

City	War loan	City	War loan
Birmingham	£6,250,239	Hull	Exact figure not reported but just under £2,000,000
Manchester	£4,506,000	Leeds	£1,521,702
Bradford	£4,145,000	Bristol	£1,400,181
London	£3,423,264	Sheffield	£1,305,761
Newcastle	£3,032,324	Cardiff	£1,020,800
Liverpool	£2,061,012		

Generosity was not just aimed at national causes. Sir James Reckitt bought Northlands, Walkington, to establish a farm colony for persons who had sufficiently recovered from T.B. to be sent to complete their cure.

As in previous Januarys there was news of another naval loss. HMS *Racoon* was a Beagle class, three funnelled coal burning destroyer. During the early hours of 9 January 1918 she was en route from Liverpool to Lough Swilly to take up anti-submarine and convoy duties in the Northern Approaches, in heavy sea conditions. While experiencing snow blizzards, she struck rocks at the Garvan Isles and sank with the loss of all hands. The only survivors were those who had been left behind at the last port of call. However, Captain Wilson's release from a POW camp was a real cause for celebration.

In summer 1917, a leading Hull butcher had forecast problems with meat availability. Since then the situation had worsened. Only a few days into the New Year, only twenty per cent of the normal weekly meat arrived in Hull. The decision was taken that all butchers, including pork butchers, would close on Monday and Tuesday during the crisis. They asked the public to be economical. To further reduce the pressure on demand, many delayed cutting up meat until Saturday. In consequence of the shortage of beef and the public's eagerness to buy, many closed early or sold their mutton at a loss. Many held back their beef for the working classes on Saturday. Although it was not what was wanted, to help reduce the meat shortage 100 frozen lamb carcasses arrived in Hull. More useful was the release of 10,600lb of frozen beef suitable for boiling.

To assist families during the food shortage the council started food economy lessons. This was a four week, two-hour long, course of special demonstrations on economical cookery for mothers. Tickets were free but places had to be booked. Naturally they were run in schools.

Further help came from the Hull Food Economy Committee. In January they decided to provide a kitchen in each of the city wards to provide food for the poor working classes and the middle classes who experienced difficulty in getting food. It cost £2,000 to set the programme up. By March, two were running. At the Hessle Road kitchen, the dining area held well over 200 people and kept pigs to eat the swill, while the kitchen on Princes Avenue was set up to provide 1,000 meals.

Whilst not filling empty stomachs, a report on Germany's food shortages must have heartened Hull residents. In February they read of a report from Amsterdam about 200,000 people marching in Charlottenburg crying 'Peace! Bread!' A shot, followed by a police charge with sabres, resulted in the strikers manning barricades. From behind overturned trams, they fired and hurled projectiles at the police. Many were wounded and numerous arrests were made.

Tea was also in short supply. When it was found out that a shop in Prospect Street was selling it, a queue quickly formed. The police were soon involved but on learning that there were 700 2oz packets, they left because there was enough for everyone in the queue. The paper to wrap things in was also in short supply, with newspapers asking for first call on any supplies. Further restrictions hit newspapers and prices went up. By April the *Hull Times* was 2d a copy.

It was inevitable, needed, but not wanted by everyone. From Monday, 4 March, the new rationing cards were to be issued. The potential dilution of the meat content of sundries like sausages and pies was solved by inspectors going round the city testing them. As usual with such a volume of paperwork, it was given to teachers to deal with. An attempt was made to make the position humorous. The expectation was that there would be adverts for vegetarian boarders who could be given bags of nuts (not rationed) in return for their meat coupons.

The final air raid on Hull occurred on 12 March when *L63* made landfall over Hornsea. Following the railway line to Hull, the ship 'scattered bombs around Sutton and Swine and six within Hull.' One woman died of shock. The next attack on Hull, 12 April, fortunately missed the city by miles.

In July it was reported that 227,000 ration books had been sent out in Hull. However, some 25,000 did not receive their books because they did not apply or they simply forgot to give their address. It was not a cheap process. The first issue of ration books cost £2,500. It would have cost more if teachers had been paid the 5s an hour they asked for instead of 2s.

Rationing was about distribution and fairness, but it did not solve shortages. Earlier in the war, Hull prided itself upon the availability of land for allotments. But now land was sorely needed after the release of potato production figures. During 1917 the County of York had produced 297,000 tons but consumed 387,700, a deficit of 90,700 tons and clearly this could not continue. Lord Rhondda and agricultural expert Mr Prothero, MP, appealed to every man who had a farm, a garden or an allotment to plant more potatoes and make the county self-supporting.

Women in Hull were encouraged to join Queen Mary's Army Auxiliary Corps in order to release men for the fighting arms. Being a clerk was one aspect of the work that would eventually cover nearly every job done by a man except fighting.

In March, the government came up with a different name for collecting money voluntarily. Across the country, different names were used, but in Hull it was called Cruiser Week, because the aim was to provide enough War Loans for the government to pay for two cruisers. As usual Hull excelled, raising considerably more than the requested £800,000. The Ellerman Line purchased £1,000,000; there was an anonymous offer of £2,000,000; the Royal Insurance Company purchased £500,000; two anonymous companies purchased £350,000; £30,000 was received from the Liverpool and London War Risks

Company; the Victoria Legal Friendly Society bought £20,000 and at the Fish Dock, trawler owners, merchants and others promised £200,000. Three months later this was followed by War Weapons Week with a target of £750,000. If this sum was raised, a tank would go into action bearing Hull's name.

Easter 1918 was similar to the previous year. The weather was cold and there was little holiday spirit in Hull. Many went to church on Good Friday, in some cases to three-hour long services, and, at the Ice Citadel, General Booth conducted three services. Most picture houses were open in the afternoon and evening. As in 1917, allotment holders were out, but generally speaking, the *Hull Times* was of the opinion that not much work was done on them.

The Quakers continued to show their opposition to the war and some were prosecuted for their actions. A call to silent prayer was an unusual incident at the trial of three Quakers accused of publishing a pacifist leaflet without authority. The many Quakers in the court closed their eyes and remained in an attitude of prayer for twenty minutes while the judge considered his decision. One lady prayed aloud towards the end and no attempt was made to stop her. Harrison Burrows and Miss Edith Ellis were accused of inciting Andrew Fisher to print copies of *A Challenge to Militarism* without the name of the author or printer and without submitting it to the censor. Ellis was fined £100 and the other two received six months imprisonment. All three were ordered to pay £50 costs. A notice of appeal was given.

Another story that probably made many in Hull feel thankful about the cost of food concerned the Isle of Man. There the government could not afford to subsidise the price of a loaf of bread. It had been fixed at 10½d but was retailing at 1s.

A further National Food Kitchen was opened in June. The Porter Street kitchen was open between 8 and 9.30 am; between 11.30 am and 2 pm for dinner and from 7.30 to 9 pm for hot supper. A very popular meal, that needed no coupons and only cost 6d, was beef sausages with peas and potatoes. Porter Street provided a varied menu and allowed people to eat in or take away.

Although the weather was good at Whitsuntide, its enjoyment was curtailed by railway and food restrictions. However, many managed to get to the local coastal towns for the day or weekend. So many went that the trains were full.

To stimulate interest in War Savings, the government sent tanks around the country. They were a success. When Nelson the tank bank visited Hull in January 1918, nearly £2,000,000 was invested.

During the summer, people usually bought coal to set aside for the winter, especially as it tended to be cheaper as demand was lower. Even though it was warmer and demand was down, less was being produced due to the shortage of miners. The result was simple: prices in Hull, as in other towns, went up. In July it rose 4s in just four days.

None of the shortages or rising prices stopped Hull being a loyal and patriotic city. July was the Silver Wedding anniversary of the King and Queen. The Lord Mayor sent them a telegram: 'Loyal and hearty greetings to Your Majesties from the citizens of Hull on your Silver Wedding Day. Sincerely hoping Your Majesties may have long life and continued great happiness.'

By mid-June there was no shortage of men in the city. More and more Americans were arriving and the residents were asked to receive them as guests, with extra food provided on their rations. In the way of a welcoming gesture, a large crowd watched a basketball game between the American Army and Navy, with the winning side receiving a silver cup.

They may have been guests but they were not all angels. 'Shortly before the Armistice…a drunken member of a US naval picket started a commotion involving both civilians and British servicemen by declaring that "the Americans had come over to finish the war". The picket's comrades aggravated the situation by coming to his aid, swinging their truncheons "with a candour which is commonly reported to be the characteristic of the Police of New York City". The US Navy commander in the district justified his men's actions by arguing that the police in Hull had shown themselves unable, or unwilling, "to control its citizen mobs".'

Mention has been made of the number of women working in jobs previously considered the domain of men. Rosedowns and Thompson was a traditional engineering firm before the war. The switch to munitions and the shortage of men changed its gender structure dramatically. This is clearly shown by two snapshot dates, July 1914 and October 1918 of the number of men and women employed in the Old Foundry. During this period 212 left for service in the forces.

	Men	Women	Total
7 August 1914	273	3	276
10 October 1918	579	359	936
Break down	Under 18 117 18 - 51¼ 394 Over 51¼ 68	Under 18 13 18 – 51¼ 346	

Again the people of Hull were told how comparatively comfortable they were. In Vienna, they were informed, the daily ration was 3oz of bread and flour substitute, 1oz of meat, less than ¼oz of fat, 2½oz of potatoes, ¾oz of jam and ½oz of war coffee. The price of real food was unaffordable compared to fixed prices in Hull: 14s per lb of horseflesh and £1 13s 9d per lb for coffee.

A health disaster struck just as the future began to look less bleak. The country was hit by an epidemic of influenza. According to the papers, it did not last long in Hull but was nevertheless severe with several hundred workmen off at just one Hull works. Within a couple of weeks of the first deaths it had subsided, although there had been many cases of mortality. One example is especially poignant with three deaths in one home. In a house in Courtney Street, the mother, father and a newly-born child died. The father contracted influenza, and the wife, who was recovering from her confinement, attended him, thereby giving the disease to her child.

No matter what is going on around them, some look to the future. John Watson Logan Chambers did just that in July when he asked the council to address the housing shortage. He suggested that their seventy-five acres plan fronting the Hessle Road should be extended. Why not negotiate for the adjoining land right through to Anlaby Road from the Hull and Barnsley railway to the Pickering Road? This would give a further 150 acres and frontages on three good roads, and enable a circular tram route linking the Hessle and Anlaby Road routes.

Just three months after residents had been told that the influenza outbreak was abating, it returned with such severity that people were cautioned that they might not receive help if they did not follow the guidelines. The problem was a shortage of doctors due to military service. Those left behind were already overworked when the flu pandemic hit Hull. This meant that only the most urgent cases could be visited. To make this happen it was 'absolutely necessary that, whenever possible, messages requiring visits to be paid to patients' homes should reach the doctor before 10 o'clock in the morning.'

As well as being fatal, influenza often gave little notice, and death could follow shortly after the first symptoms. Esther Cooper, of 4 Cobden Cottages, the thirty-seven-year-old wife of a ship's carpenter, went to work on Friday 25 October. On her return from work she said: 'I think I have got a touch of the influenza, I do feel poorly.' After eating a meal she fell asleep in a chair. 'Some while afterwards her daughter found she was dead.'

Within days of the start of the Advance to Victory, thoughts turned to the future. South-west Hull MP John R. Bell wanted a number of changes. German shipping and trade should be boycotted after the war. Naval, seafaring and army men were to be established in civil life after the war. Pensions should be free of income tax and equal to pre-war earnings. He argued for housing reform, and mothers and widows to be secure, despite what they earned. Thinking far into the future, he wanted workers to have a living wage and every child to have the opportunity to advance from the elementary school to the university. Like everyone else he wanted an end to wars of aggression and, because of his background, believed that seamen and fishermen should have a direct voice in the House of Commons.

In August, during the final advances, another city councillor received sad news. His only son died of wounds aged twenty. Second

Lieutenant G.D. Gibson, educated at Hymers College and gazetted from Sandhurst to the 5th Lancers, was shot in the head during a cavalry charge.

Even though the end was in sight, money was still needed to help soldiers. During August, the Hull and East Riding Fund for the Needs of Local Units and PoWs, headquartered in Peel House on Beverley Road, appealed for funds. There were, by then, over 1,000 men in captivity with more names being added every day. It was costing £34 2s 6d for each PoW. Sponsors who would adopt a prisoner were needed. Books were also needed for hospitals and camp libraries in France.

Only days away from the end of the war, Peter Gaskell became the new Lord Mayor of Hull. In his inaugural speech he espoused his ideas for the post-war future. He wanted the city to construct 'wide new imposing boulevards jutting miles out from Hull into the countryside.' Each would be 'fittingly named as a lasting memorial to commemorate the battles and events in which Hull men took part in the great struggle for right and liberty.' As an architect he was keen to improve Hull's housing, which was 5,000 short, rising by 1,200 per annum. Like the MP for South-west Hull, he had a vision of a brighter future. He wanted a 'holistic approach that included industrial building, as well as social, industrial such as workshops and factories. There should be proper light and ventilation and sanitary equipment, where men and women follow their avocations.' He wanted the days of long streets to be replaced by estates of groups of six to eight houses with abundant space for air, light and sun.

Throughout the war, escaped Germans had been roaming through the country. The last escapees had been no closer than Scarborough. Suddenly, in mid-October, there was one in Hull. After escaping from Catterick Camp on 19 August, Johannen von Gruber, described as a dangerous German, moved around. The forty-five-year-old arrived by train from London and spent the night in a hotel registered as a British citizen before being detained and sent back to Catterick. At the time of his escape he was classed 'as a man dangerous to the country while free. He had shown ingenuity when he cleared the camp by exchanging places with a unit attached to a working road party, later escaping the vigilance of the guards over the road party, and subsequently leaving Catterick by train.'

Even with victory looming, Hull received news that there would be a meat shortage in 1919, at its worst in May and June before summer grazing fattened cattle. There was no assistance from Ireland as imports had been restricted, but this was good news for the Irish as they had a meat glut. Again the issue was shipping. Australia had an abundance of beef available and New Zealand had millions of sheep carcasses ready to send. On the bright side, for the Christmas market, a normal allotment of beasts was indicated, with the authorities trying to increase it.

With increasing numbers of air raids, a charity was formed to help those affected. This is an example of a Flag Day pin.

By November it was becoming obvious that the fighting would stop but this did not prevent Withernsea organising a Guns Week savings campaign for February 1919. This was at the same time that women working in munitions were being given a week's wage in lieu of notice when dismissed from employment.

Then came news of an armistice. Everywhere celebrated victory in their own way. In Cottingham, Hallgate was decorated all week. On the Market Green, youths burned an effigy of the Kaiser and set off crackers and small bombs. In the evening there was a thanksgiving service in the church. At Windsor, the King celebrated victory during dinner with champagne.

KEEP THIS BY YOU FOR REFERENCE.   N.R. 1. (Nov.)

MINISTRY OF FOOD. Rationing Order, 1918.
(These instructions are additional to those printed in the Ration Book Itself.)

1. If any book is sent to your house which you cannot deliver to its owner, send it back at once to your Food Office with a note explaining why it cannot be delivered.
2. Read the instructions on the cover of your ration book carefully, and in accordance with them :—
    (a) Sign your name and write your address on the cover of the book, on the reference leaf and on each page of coupons.
    (b) Take your book at once to each retailer with whom you are already registered and get him to enter his name and address in the proper space on the back of the cover. You must not change your retailer without the written consent of the Food Office.
3. JAM. You must register before November 10th with a retailer for jam. To do this you must fill up the Spare Counterfoil (iv.) leaf 5 (red). The retailer will enter his name and address on the proper space (No. 7) on the back cover and will detach and keep the counterfoil.
    Jam, marmalade, syrup, treacle, and honey will be rationed as from November 3rd, on the red coupons on leaf 5 marked "spare." You can buy jam and marmalade on these coupons only from the retailer with whom you are registered. You can buy syrup, treacle and honey on these coupons from any retailer who can supply you.
    Persons who will be between the ages of 6 and 18 at midnight on the 31st December next can obtain a supplementary ration of jam. These persons will receive a book containing an extra leaf of red coupons (Leaf 5x) with a counterfoil marked "Jam counterfoil" (supplementary). They must register this counterfoil, as well as the spare counterfoil (iv.), leaf 5, with a jam retailer.
            INSTRUCTIONS IN CASE OF REMOVALS.
4. Always take your Ration Book with you if you go to stay away from home.
    If you have deposited any leaves of coupons with retailers, collect them before you start your journey.
    If you are removing permanently (see paragraph 6), you must, before starting, collect the counterfoils which you gave up from your old ration book when you registered with your retailers. If the retailer informs you that they are at the Food Office, you need not collect them but must tell the Food Office of the district to which you are moving.
            TEMPORARY REMOVALS.
5. If you are going to stay in a hotel, boarding house, canteen, etc., you can use your ration book there without any formalities.
    If you are going to stay in a private house or lodgings, you will be able, so far as
3477. Wt.   /F526. 6,000,000(96). 8/18 S.O.,F.Rd.

The instructions for the new ration cards.

MINISTRY OF FOOD.

NATIONAL RATION BOOK (B).

INSTRUCTIONS.

Read carefully these instructions and the leaflet which will be sent you with this Book.

1. The person named on the reference leaf as the holder of this ration book must write his name and address in the space below, and must write his name and address, and the serial number (printed upside down on the back cover), in the space provided to the left of each page of coupons.

Food Office of } Issue .... **Beverley Rural** .... 19 OCT 1918 Date ....

Signature of Holder .... *Laurence Binnington* ....

Address .... *Walkington* ....

2. For convenience of writing at the Food Office the Reference Leaf has been put opposite the back cover, and has purposely been printed upside down. It should be carefully examined. If there is any mistake in the entries on the Reference Leaf, the Food Office should be asked to correct it.

3. The holder must register this book at once by getting his retailers for butcher's meat, bacon, butter and margarine, sugar and tea respectively, to write their names and the addresses of their shops in the proper space on the back of the cover. Persons staying in hotels, boarding houses, hostels, schools, and similar establishments should not register their books until they leave the establishment.

4. The ration book may be used only by or on behalf of the holder, to buy rationed food for him, or members of the same household, or guests sharing common meals. It may not be used to buy rationed food for any other persons.

N. 2 J (Nov.)

(Continued on next page.

(left margin:) IF FOUND, RETURN TO ANY FOOD OFFICE.

The front cover of a ration book issued to Laurence Binnington of Walkington.

From the

Chancellor of The Exchequer

to YOU.

The Food to which these Ration Books relate is available for you only because the British Fleet guards our transport of food from the distant shores where it is produced. To keep the ocean highways open—to protect food-ships that must come in their thousands if we are to live and win—the Navy must be maintained and sustained.

And to win the military victory that must come before peace is possible, the Army and the Royal Air Force must be kept at full strength—provided generously with the weapons and engines of defence and offence.

For these purposes your country needs you to lend your money—not to give it—only to lend it on very profitable terms. This is the duty required of every man and

woman here at home—of all of us who, by age or physical weakness or the nature of our work, are held back from actual service with the Colours.

Six things we can do—and should do if we would be worthy of the sacrifices brave men are making for us.

(1) Lives must be lived more simply.

(2) Personal, household and business expenses must be reduced to the minimum.

(3) The surplus of weekly or monthly earnings over necessary expenditure must be invested straightway in National War Bonds or War Savings Certificates.

(4) Current balances at the bank should be kept as small as possible, and the money invested in National War Bonds as and when it comes in.

(5) Private individuals with money on deposit in banks should withdraw as much as they can and invest it in National War Bonds.

(6) Business people and firms with money on deposit should withdraw all not absolutely needed for their business operations and invest it in National War Bonds.

The whole nation is, I am convinced, more determined now than at any time since the struggle began that the War must end in a victorious Peace. To secure this victory, our people do not hesitate to risk, and indeed to give, their own lives and the lives of those dear to them; they will not hesitate to lend their money.

34D. Wt. 21,444/2734. 3,100,000(30). 8/18. S.O.,F.Rd.

A message from the Chancellor of the Exchequer explaining the need for rationing and asking people to lend their money to the government.

The next day the *Hull Daily Mail* described the previous day's events. 'At all the big works in East Hull, at Earle's Shipyard, and at the docks, the workpeople took holiday. When the news was received, the men decided upon "going home", and they put on their coats and left work...Munition girls joined the crowds of school children and perambulated the main street in a jubilant spirit. The shops selling small flags were doing a roaring trade, and they sold out several times during the morning. Some of the rejoicers provided themselves with musical instruments and some had bells. Although no arrangements were made to close schools many children took a holiday. By 3 pm Mr. Cook of the Corporation Gas Department had started scraping the paint off lamps. Church bells commenced to ring from 3 pm onwards. Even the GPO decked the counter railings with small flags. Soldiers at a local camp were given leave for the day.'

The *Hull Times* was more emotional. 'Was there ever such a day as yesterday? I think not in the memory of any living person. Throughout, the day was marked by scenes of enthusiasm that were almost beyond the power of anyone to set down in cold type...when the news was sent out that the armistice had been signed...the crowds commenced to give way to their enthusiasm and relieve their pent-up feelings...the ringing of church bells and the chiming of public clocks that have been silent for long told their own story. But what struck one most was the lights after tea..."Lights," was the cry on Monday evening, and as if the illuminations of the street lamps, the shops, and the public buildings were not enough, fireworks of all descriptions were used.'

To enhance the celebrations, the Home Office allowed shops lights for the day. It must have been disappointing for the outgoing mayor not to be involved in the celebrations after he had guided the city through the war. It was the first business day for the new mayor who announced the armistice and the peace that would follow. In the Council Chamber at 11.45 am, the councillors rose to their feet and sang the National Anthem. Outside, many fireworks were being let off.

At 3 pm the buzzers sounded the all clear and at 6 pm searchlights lit the sky and a military band started to play outside the City Hall. Although the crowds were large, with rockets, fog signals being set off and dancing in the streets, the celebrations were masked by restraint with the whole atmosphere being 'redolent of sheer happiness'.

With victory achieved, the death of a loved one must have been especially poignant; the end of the war did not stop the dying, and as usual the *Hull Daily Mail* carried a Roll of Honour that included deaths in action and deaths from wounds and illness. On a day of victory what must it have felt like to place notice of the funeral of your only son? Private Frederick Soulsby, aged eighteen, had died in the Military Hospital in Clipstone Camp. His funeral cortege would leave his home, 135 Westcott Street, on 14 November for burial in Hedon Road Cemetery. The next day the Roll of Honour included Private Norton, who had been wounded and had to have both legs amputated.

Losses must be even worse when they are not officially recognised: J. Sawney, RE, of 57 Albany Street, accidentally drowned on 16 December, aged eighteen; G. Millest died on active service aged twenty-seven on 4 December; and Watson Gathercole, aged twenty-eight, who died as the result of gas poisoning, were not listed as deaths by the CWGC.

Countering this was some good news. Sergeant and Mrs George Cox of 216 Marlborough Avenue were proud to announce the birth of their son on 12 November.

Although the war was over, the East Yorkshire Volunteer Regiment would continue on into 1919 before it was stood down. On 11

Female employees at the Smith & Nephew factory on Tadman Street in 1918. From left to right back row: Doris Bell, Blanche Chapman, Mary Keenan. Front row: Lilian Brazier and Gladys Brown.

November its strength was considerable and also unique. It was the only county regiment to offer so many specialist units together in one force and fielded the only horse transport unit in Britain.

	Officers	Ranks
RGA 2 Companies	6	132
RE 3 units	12	211
Infantry 4 battalions	106	3201*
RASC (MT)	12	246
RASC (HT)	18	165
RAMC 4 Field Ambulances	6	246

*Included 4 Anti-aircraft guns in Hull.

Within days of the signing of the Armistice, thoughts turned to demobilisation from the forces. A priority release scheme for the army was put into effect. Employers in Hull, holding posts vacant for the return of serving officers or men of similar educational standing, and wishing to apply for their priority release, were urged to write to the directorate in the Hull region at the Appointments Department, Ministry of Labour, in Leeds.

One of those returning home now the war was over was Max Schultz. Hull's spy had been released before the war ended, but because of the dangerous situation in Germany it was safer in prison than out of it. True to his beliefs, in his days of relative freedom he had continued to spy, and, on his return on 26 November, reported to Military Intelligence. Sometime after this he returned to his family in Coltman Street.

Along with early release came news of the repatriation of PoWs, with Hull as a selected port of return. The first steamer to arrive was the *Archangel*, which brought home 1,000 men. By Christmas, nearly 39,000 had arrived at the port.

About 70,000 men and women from Hull and the immediate surrounding area had served in the armed forces, about 7,000 people, including civilians, from Hull were killed and over 14,000 seriously wounded or disabled. To assist then, The Hull War Trust was set up to raise funds and by 1927 1,040 recipients had received £74,000.

The packing of parcels by The Hull and East Riding Fund for the needs of Local Units and Prisoners of War was stopped on Wednesday, 13 November, shortly before it was announced that many prisoners would return via Hull. In response to this, 'General Sir Stanley von Donop, commanding the Humber Garrison, asked Lady Nunburnholme to get together a group of ladies to welcome the men on their arrival at the Riverside Quay. Peel House workers all volunteered to help, and from November 17th, when the first boat arrived, to the 31st January, when the last boat delivered its load, the ladies attended regularly, in shifts of twelve to meet the men. They helped the Navy and Army Canteen Board by distributing their "Luxury Parcels" for them, and they also distributed newspapers, postcards and pencils. The newspapers were supplied free by the *London Daily Mail, The Daily Chronicle*, and the local *Hull News* and the *Daily Mail*, and they were much appreciated by officers and men alike. The postcards were collected again before the trains left the station, and posted for the men. Sometimes, in the case of officers, telegrams were taken to the G.P.O. and despatched for them. Later, when the "Luxury Parcels" were put on board the ships at the other side, Peel House distributed cigarettes, and also gave each man a card of instructions from the Central Prisoners of War Committee.'

The news of victory was tinged with sadness for many, but especially for the families of those who died as the war was ending. Corporal E. Shanks, eldest son of Mrs Shanks of 38 Morpeth Street, serving in the RFA, died on 7 November, from wounds received on 1 November. He had only returned to France on 17 October after fourteen days' leave.

Illness was now a major killer at home and abroad. Twenty-five-year-old Bombardier Arthur Marr was at home on leave when he developed septic pneumonia. He died at home on 11 November after serving with the Hull Heavy Battery for the whole of the war. He was the youngest son of Mr and Mrs T.J. Marr of 79 Constable Street. On the same day, thirty-year-old Lieutenant R.G. Guthrie of the RFA was buried at Northern Cemetery with full military honours. During the fighting at Ypres he was gassed, contracted trench fever and was invalided home. He was under orders to return to the Front when he caught influenza and pneumonia supervened. He was married with one child. East Yorkshire Volunteer Regiment Private H. Pinder of 1a Selby Street, died at home and was buried in Western Cemetery. Twenty-one-year-old Private William Shanks, a Hull postman from 33 Hopwood Street, was serving in the MGC when he returned to France on 6 November. He died of bronchial pneumonia at Boulogne on 12 December.

Lloyd George called an election immediately after victory. It was the first to be held after the Representation of the People Act 1918, which meant it was the first United Kingdom general election in which any women could vote. It was also the first in which all men over the age of 21 could vote; previously many poor or Catholic men had been excluded from voting, while the new laws still excluded women under the age of 30. It was also the first election to be held on a single day. Sir Mark Sykes stood as the Coalition Unionist and Colonel Lambert-Ward was adopted as the Unionist candidate. Polling was to take place on 14 December, with counting taking place much later, to allow 29,797 absent voters' papers to be counted. Absent voter totals show a similarity in contribution of men from the ward to the war, except the South-west ward: East – 7,043; North-west – 7,132; Central – 7,283; South-west – 8,339. In total 126,755 people voted.

Voting over, thoughts could turn to the first Christmas of peace for five years. Keeping warm was always an issue and Hull residents were no doubt pleased when they found out that emergency supplies of coal were being brought in so there was enough for the festive season. For the poor who could not afford to buy enough, The Mother Humber Fund received forty tons as a gift from Messrs W.A. Massey and Co. for free distribution to those in need.

Although prisoners were being repatriated and some men released early, most would continue in the armed forces for months until the peace was certain. Once again, money was needed.

Towards the end of 1916, Lord and Lady Nunburnholme had issued an appeal to the public for funds to provide Christmas comforts for the officers and men associated with Hull and East Riding units serving overseas. The response was immediate and in one day over £1,000 was collected. For the remaining Christmases of the war, the fund was taken over by the Lord Mayor.

The level of contribution in military terms that Hull made to the war effort, without taking into account the men in the navy and air force, is shown by the length of the list of gifts the Lord Mayor sent at Christmas 1918.

Unit	Amount £-s-d	Unit	Amount £-s-d
1st Bn. East Yorks	100-0-0	146th (Hull) Heavy	25-0-0
2nd Bn. East Yorks	100-0-0	77th Siege Battery RGA	25-0-0
6th Bn. East Yorks	100-0-0	164th Siege Battery RGA	25-0-0
7th Bn. East Yorks	125-0-0	32nd Divisional Ammun. Column RFA	50-0-0
10th Bn. East Yorks	125-0-0	251st Brigade RFA	25-0-0
11th Bn. East Yorks	100-0-0	102nd Bn MGC	50-0-0
2/4th Bn. East Yorks	100-0-0	1/1st East Riding Field Coy RE	25-0-0
1st Garrison Bn. East Yorks	100-0-0	1/3rd Northumbrian RAMC	20-0-0
31st Machine Gun Bn.	25-0-0	545th Heavy Battery RGA	25-0-0
1/3rd Coy Northumbrian RE	25-0-0	47th Brigade RFA	10-0-0
2/3rd Coy Northumbrian RE	20-0-0	256th Siege Battery RFA	10-0-0
124th (Hull) Heavy Battery RGA	25-0-0		
		Total	1,230-0-0

On Christmas Eve, the *Hull Daily Mail* wrote that 'the rosy sunrise of Christmas Eve seemed a veritable sign and portent of the changed time in which we are spending what had been described very happily as "the Greatest Christmas since the first".' With it came a sense of relief and the hope for a better world.

According to the *Hull Times* it 'was certainly the happiest "festive season" the British Empire' had enjoyed, 'certainly since the war broke out. Trade in the shops was of "record" dimensions and the street afforded innumerable evidences of the freedom from care and anxiety and the passing of the war strain from the people. The military and other hospitals and all the charitable institutions were scenes of brightness and festivity.'

It is doubtful if this brightness was shared by those who had recently lost a loved one. For them, it must have been a time of very mixed emotions. Imagine what it must have been like for Mr and Mrs

Private Ernest Bogg of Hull, who was killed serving with the 2nd/5th Lincolnshire Regiment in 1918.

G. Littledike, a Hull resident, was killed in action on 2 September 1918 serving with the Shropshire Light Infantry.

Now 18, Harold Cook received his call-up papers. Within days he was training at Clipstone. Although demobilised on 11 November he volunteered for regular service and was soon fighting in Iraq.

BRILLIANT HULL AIRMAN.

Second-Lieutenant A. Birrell, aged 24 years, pilot, Royal Air Forces, was killed whilst flying in France on the 18th inst. He was the youngest son of Mr and Mrs W. A. Birrell, of 44, Park-street, Hull, and the second out of three who have made the supreme sacrifice in France, the eldest being killed in January, 1915.

Lieutenant A. Birrell has had a brilliant career. In one of his military courses he passed with distinction, and was placed first in the whole of the British Isles. In another course he came out second in the British Isles. He was an athlete of considerable repute, having held both swimming and boxing championships. Being mobilised as a Territorial at the outbreak of the war, he has served his country since August, 1914. His Squadron Commander describes him as a man of great promise.

The third son is a commissioned officer in the Royal Engineers.

After surviving as an infantryman on the Western Front from early 1915, Second Lieutenant Birrell transferred to the RAF and trained as a pilot. He was serving with 13 Squadron when he was killed on 18 September 1918.

By November 1918 military funerals no longer attracted onlookers. This is the funeral procession for twenty-six-year-old Private John Mann. He had joined the 13th (4th City) Battalion in December 1914 and served throughout the war, dying at home on 16 November.

Hutchinson that Christmas. They had lost their eldest son in Palestine and were waiting for their other son, a PoW, to return home. There was no news of his return and then a friend of Edmund's in the camp made contact. This friend had kept a secret diary in which were details of the PoWs' life and treatment. It also contained the story of their son's death. He had been murdered by a German sentry. On 21 October he was accused of smoking a cigarette on parade and set upon by a sentry who beat him so unmercifully that he died that night.

What sort of Christmas was it for the parents of Signaller George Clinton of D Company, 1st Battalion East Yorks, Charles Edward and Elizabeth, or his wife Fanny Clinton, of 15 Horace Avenue? They were informed he had died in Gosforth Hospital on 12 December. The war had been over for a month and he was in his fifth year of service.

With the war ending, grouped losses were even more poignant.

HULL MERCANTILE MARINE OFFICER WRECKED.

The friends and relatives of Mr and Mrs W. Rutter, 120, Londesborough-street, Hull, will be pleased to learn that their only son, Douglas J. Rutter, who was wrecked off Key West on the s.s. Bayreuto, on September 12th, has been landed safe at Havana. The first reports stated that a number of men were missing, but Mr Rutter was saved, along with the master and 16 other members of the crew. A later report states that all the crew are safe. Mr Rutter was 3rd officer on board the vessel which sailed from Plymouth in August. He is an old Trinity House boy

PRIVATE F. TURNER.

Pte. F. Turner (60841), 1st East Yorks Regt., reported missing on September 10th, 1918, now officially reported killed on or about that date. Previous to joining the Colours he worked for Mr H. Field, Billingsgate. He served in Egypt and France since November, 1914, and was formerly in the 4th Hull Pals' Battalion. Any further news would be gratefully received by his parents at 50, Railway cottages, Dairycoates, Hessle-road, Hull.

A rather unfortunate coupling of stories: one saved, the other presumed dead.

The Reading Room at the Soldier's Club in Hull.

CHAPTER 6

1919:
The Homecoming

With no war, restrictions on celebrations were fewer, allowing New Year festivities. In pre-war years such indulgences would have passed without comment but, after years of frugality and restriction, the *Hull Daily Mail* felt duty bound to comment. 'Certainly 1919 starts under the auspices of hope and there was some reason for the rather noisy manifestations of rejoicing in London, Leeds and Hull at midnight. The reaction after a great strain has been so profound that it would be strange if we returned to the normal and the formal in a moment and the wonder is not so much that many people, "raised a key above themselves", should spend such large sums of money and precious time upon "celebrations" such as those that took place in London and many provincial hotels last night, but that the nation, as a whole, should be sober in its hour of triumph.'

The *Eastern Daily News* was more upbeat about the first New Year of peace. 'The New Year – the year of Peace – was heralded in Hull in pre-war fashion. Bells rang out their merry peals and buzzers blew their blatant blasts, which were interpreted as the "All Clear" not only from passing danger but from war alarms for ever. Churches and chapels were filled with larger congregations than usual, and the youngsters showering their wishes and soliciting coppers seemed to be everywhere. The weather had cleared, a wet day being followed by a fine and frosty night.'

Its editorial was one of hope. 'The hope that springs eternal in the human breast is active in our breasts today, as we start this new year of 1919 free from the darkening shadow of war. Our hope is that we have left behind for ever our days of horror and gloom, and that hence forward our years may be cheered by benignant brightness. We enter upon this period with feelings that differ vastly from those which were in our minds when, twelve months ago, we hailed the dawn of an opening year.'

As the people of Hull started the first day of the New Year, a day of peace, news came of one of the worst peacetime maritime disaster to dates. HMS *Iolaire* was carrying sailors back to the Scottish island of Lewis. She left the port of Kyle of Lochalsh on the mainland late on the evening of the 31 December 1918. But, at 2.30 am on New Year's Day, as the ship approached the port of Stornoway, a few yards offshore and a mile away from the safety of Stornoway Harbour, she hit the infamous rocks The Beasts of Holm and eventually sank. The final death toll was officially put at 205, of whom 181 were islanders, but as the ship was badly overcrowded and there was a lack of proper records the death toll might well have been slightly higher. John F. Macleod from Ness, Isle of Lewis, saved 40 lives, swimming ashore with a heaving line, along which many of the survivors made their way to safety. Only 75 of the 280 (officially known) passengers survived the disaster; 73 per cent perished in the incident.

The East Yorkshire Volunteer Regiment provided the greatest range of arms of service of the volunteers in the country. This is the Army Service Corps being inspected towards the end of the war.

Hull was a potential target for air raids: volunteer units like this were used in its defence.

Shipping losses were not confined to the Royal Navy. Before the New Year the Wilson Line ship *Gitano* had disappeared. It had been seen off Flamborough Head and then nothing. Posted as missing, and in fact sunk after hitting a mine, its wreckage was washed up in Norway. Many of the missing were from Hull and district.

Stationers were quick to produce victory goods.

There was some good news to start the year. There would be no ration books once supplies had been stabilised. Hammonds announced its sale and, even more importantly, the Ministry of Food submitted plans for better and cheaper beer. There were further improvements to the life of the average Hull family. Onions were to be cheaper, more tinned salmon was to be made available and the butter and margarine ration was to be increased to 6oz.

With so much captured enemy hardware, it was decided to award trophies to cities in acknowledgement of their contribution to the war effort. It was decided that Hull should receive ten German field guns and these arrived in January at Londesborough Street Barracks. Four had been captured on 2 September by 1st East Yorkshire Regiment, two 105mm howitzers and two 77mm field guns. Viewers contributed to the VAD hospitals to see the guns. One of the guns had been captured

The first ships carrying repatriated PoWs were the SS Archangel *and SS* Stockport. *They arrived from Rotterdam on 17 November carrying 1,700 men.*

by 237 Battalion CEF and was inscribed 'Captured and claimed by the 27th Canadian Battalion. To go to the Lieutenant Governor Manitoba, Canada.' What happened to these guns? One of them was on sale at an antique shop on Beverley Road in the 1970s. Where did it go?

Families with loved ones still officially listed as missing drew some hope of resolution from the large numbers of newly-arrived POWs. In the same edition of the *Hull Times* were thirteen requests for information. The following is typical. 'The parents of Private J. W. (Jack) Kirk, 11/51 11th East Yorks, who reside in Knight Street, Barton, would be glad of any information concerning him. He was reported missing on March 27th last year, near Oppy Wood, and in spite of constant inquiries nothing further has been heard of him. It is thought some of the repatriated prisoners may be able to give some information.'

Among those returning should have been Rifleman Ambrose Bottomley, an employee at Fargas Oil Mills in Wincolmlee. He had been a PoW in Germany since October 1915 and his wife and three children looked forward to his arrival at any time. Early in the New Year they received notification that he would not return. After a short illness, he had died of heart failure on 17 November in Germany before he could be released.

While some clung to hope, most realised that the missing would not return. Even by the time of the peace celebrations, there were still death notifications appearing in the press.

With the influenza epidemic over, the Corporation published information on its effects locally and across the nation. 'The widespread epidemic of flu in this country in June and July 1918 was followed after a short interval by a second wave of prevalence during October, November and December of the same year. A third wave of considerable magnitude occurred in the following February and March.'

During the summer outbreak, in the ninety-six great towns in England and Wales, estimated population 16,577,344, during the seven weeks from 22 June to 10 August, the number of deaths ran at 29.3 per 100,000 – 4,894 people, not including death by pneumonia. The second wave was more lethal. Between 12 October and 28 December it killed 44,537, 269 per 100,000. In some towns it ran at 400 per 100,000. Between 1 February and 5 April it fell to 17,219 deaths

Pte. C. WHITELOCK.   A. YOUNG.

Mrs C. Whitelock, 8, Dorset-street, Gipsyville, was officially informed on Thursday that her son, Private Charles Whitelock, who left Hull on March 14th, was killed in action on March 21st, 1918. Private Whitelock was 29 years of age, and was employed by Messrs Blazier and Carr, fish curers, before joining up.

Sad news has been received by Mrs Young, 40, Eton-street, that her husband, Arthur Young, mate on H.M.T. ——, which was sunk in collision on October 29th, has been lost, after serving four years. Before the war he sailed for years as boatswain in Wilson and Ellerman Line. He was in the s.s. Ebro in the Messina earthquake in 1908, and received a silver medal from the King of Italy for taking part in the life-saving operations. Deceased was 34 years of age, and leaves a widow and two little sons to mourn the loss.

For some parents it was months before their son's death was confirmed, for others the news was almost immediate. In November the Hull Times *reported the deaths of a soldier in March and a sailor in October.*

G. D. BARRASS.   Pte. H. SELLERS.

George Downing Barrass, deck hand, R.N.R., who died in the Royal Naval Hospital Pembroke Dock, from influenza and toxaemia, at the age of 28. He leaves a wife and two children, who reside at 42, Marmaduke-street, Hull.

The sad news has been received of the death in action on October 8th, 1918, of Pte. Herbert A. Sellers, Northumberland Fusiliers. He volunteered at the age of 15, but on his correct age being discovered, he was not called up until he attained the age of 18. He was wounded in France last May, and had only been out again three weeks, when he met his death. He was not then 19. Previous to enlisting he was a clerk at Messrs Grant and Co., Paragon-street Hull.

With the war obviously about to end any loss was especially sad but probably more so when it was caused by illness just days before the Armistice.

or 104 per 100,000. Young adults were especially affected by the pandemic with the largest proportion of deaths being people under forty-five. There had been similar epidemics in 1803, 1833, 1837, 1847 and 1890.

How had Hull fared during this period? The Medical Officer of Health reported that for the four-week period ended 31 August there had been just three flu deaths, thirteen deaths from pneumonia and eleven from bronchitis with one, thirteen and fifteen deaths respectively in September; the same levels as the previous year. The three weeks ending 19 October showed a worsening situation – numbers in brackets are the percentage of total deaths.

Week ending	Total deaths	Respiratory Organ disease (influenza, pneumonia and bronchitus	Influenza	Pneumonia	Bronchitus
5 October	59	11 (18.6)	1 (1.7)	8 (13.5)	2 (3.3)
12 October	89	25 (28)	14 (15.7)	8 (8.9)	3 (3.3)
19 October	166	104 (62.6)	69 (41.6)	24 (14.4)	11 (6.6)

Total deaths of 166 in a week equated to an annual rate of 35.3 per thousand, against 15.1 and 12.8 in the preceding two weeks.

Some areas of Hull were worse affected. During the week ending 19 October, forty-seven of the sixty-nine deaths occurred in East Sculcoates (17 deaths) and West Sculcoates (30 deaths). There was also a difference in the ages affected. Nearly half (thirty-four) of the deaths were in the age range 25 to 45, then 5 to 15 (eighteen) and over 65 only five deaths.

By Easter the worst was over and the papers reported a drop in the death rate. In the ninety-six great towns of England and Wales, it dropped from the beginning to the end of March from 35.7 to 19.3. Birkenhead recorded a drop from 16 to 9 in one week and thirteen towns recorded a rate under 29 but one town, Ipswich, showed an increase from 20.81 to 23. Like Leeds and Newcastle, Hull recorded a rate of 18, higher than Huddersfield and York but lower than Sunderland and Bradford.

A further health issue brought to light after the war was sexually transmitted disease. The Hull Venereal Disease clinic had treated 522 people during 1918, nearly all of these being residents. In a port the size of Hull, with thousands of sailors passing through, it is surprising that only fifty-four seamen were treated, just ten per cent of the cases. The most disease needing treatment was syphilis, 305 cases, gonorrhoea, 183 cases and soft chancre, 35 cases. No comment about the effectiveness of the treatment was made or any information on whether any had contracted the disease more than once.

There was no longer the same need for charity and many organisations were wound up. One such group was the Belgian Refugees Committee which issued its final Report in April. It had assisted 1,249 refugees, of whom 612 were entertained and 637 given temporary material aid. Through collections, contributions, donations and sales it had raised £10,386 6s 8¾d that was used to assist and maintain refugees and their repatriation.

On a larger scale, organisations like The Hull and East Riding Fund for the needs of Local Units and Prisoners of War were also wound up. The final reports show the scale of the work undertaken in Hull. The fund had been approved by the War Office and registered under the War Charities Act of 1916 with headquarters at Peel House, 28, Beverley Road, Hull. The Presidents were Lord and Lady Nunburnholme, the Lord Mayor of Hull, Major General Sir Coleridge and Colonel Stacey-Clitherow. Mr W.F. Harris was the chairman of the central committee, assisted by ninety-two trustees. The organisation began its activities just before the war on 2 August 1914 when Peel House was opened by the Presidents, Lord and Lady Nunburnholme. Its scope was extended from time to time as necessity arose and its activities continued ceaselessly until 31 January 1919, when the last boat-load of repatriated prisoners arrived at the Riverside Quay. During this period, local support had been very generous and the fund finished in profit. At the cessation of its role, this excess was given to the Central Prisoners of War Committee. Its final report showed how much work had been done.

Précis of work done 1914 –1918

	1914/15	1915/16	1916/17	1917/19	Total
Number of articles despatched to East Riding troops	24,854	38,221	34,389	12,436	109,000
Number of parcels (food and clothing) sent to PoWs	147	7,200	54,000	69,994	131,341
Number of men passed through rest station (day and night)	27,840	108,741	302,800	326,225	765,606
Number of hospital supplies despatched	4,729	9,100	22,426	115,784	152,039
St John VAD hospital: out-patients attended and in-patients treated, 1917 to 1919	Out patients attendances (1917) 2,739	In patients attendances (1917) 1,620	Out patients attendances (1918) 41,940	In patients attendances (1918) 2,774	In patients/ out patients 4,394/ 44,679

Monies collected 1914 – 1918

	1914/15 £	1915/16 £	1916/17 £	1917/18 £	1918/19 £	Total £
Collected for "Comforts fund"	1,837	5,477	2,516	132	171	10,133
Collected for Prisoners of War fund	-----	1,960	10,862	27,951	14,855	55,628
Receipts, &c. at "Rest Station"	117	109	900	2,196	923	4,245
Collected for hospital supplies fund	-----	776	686	786	-----	2,248
Collected for St John VAD hospital	-----	-----	14,935	7,686	-----	22,621
Collected for Christmas funds	-----	1,421	1,435	1,230	-----	4,136
Totals	1,954	9,743	31,384	39,981	15,949	99,011

As well as providing the necessaries of life for local Prisoners of war there was also a "Comforts Fund" for Hull and East Riding troops that was independent from the fund run by the East Yorkshire regiment for its two regular battalions.

E. S. 1493. WIMEREUX (P.-de-C.)
L'Avenue de la Mer

A postcard from a Hull soldier telling his parents that he will be home soon.

The "Comforts Fund" depots had been set up 'to provide extras to local men serving at home and abroad and also to aid the VAD Hospital in Hull. Volunteer helpers, often over 70 years of age, undertook the cutting out, machining and fixing of shirts, the packaging of warm clothing and socks for the troops. When military demand was not high, they made hospital garments such as flannel under-vests and pants, and also repaired clothing and bed and table linen, for the VAD hospital. Wool was distributed to home workers to make items such as socks and mufflers. Between 1 January and 31 October 1918, the depot received 4,129 articles from sources as diverse as the Guildhall working party, the Hornsea working party, Canon England, Mrs Savory and Friends, and the Craven Street Girls' School. During this same period they despatched 3,452 articles to destinations as diverse as the

VAD hospital on Cottingham Road, the Military hospital in Middlesborough, Reckitt's hospital, Colonel Wilkinson (500 pairs of socks), Mr Rippon (two pairs of socks) and a soldier's wife (one pair of socks). Twenty-two different types of goods were despatched, the most numerous being socks (1,760 pairs); the other articles sent out were 367 shirts, 69 pairs of pants, 16 cardigans, 235 comfort bags, 281 pairs of mitts, 7 pairs of gloves, 198 mufflers, 214 helmets, 55 operation stockings, 4 belts, 56 vests, 1 pair of boots, 6 handkerchiefs, 38 bed jackets, 1 dish cloth, 2 chest protectors, 1 tin cover, 125 face washers, 12 cushions, 2 bandages and 2 Housewifes. Over roughly the same period (1 January to 30 September), the Beverley War Depot and the East Riding War Depot received 3,492 articles and despatched 4,650. Like the Hull depot, the most common article to be despatched were socks (4,600 pairs). During the same period, the Beverley depot also sent out 1,430 articles to hospitals. Sub-depots at Rise, Bridlington, Cottingham, Welton, Norton and Settrington contributed articles to the main Beverley depot.'

To finance this work, the War Depot received money from the Hull and East Riding War Needs Fund, donations and self-generated income from the sale of teas. From 14 November 1917 to 31 October 1918, including bank interest, this amounted to £216-17s-8d; outgoings during the same period left just over £95 in the bank.

Requisitions supplied from the War Depots
from January 1918 to 1919

Unit	Socks	Shirts	Helmets	Mufflers	Pants and vests	Miscellaneous
4th East Yorks, 1st line	500	35		50	20	
7th East Yorks	500	926		125		Hockey sticks and balls for 92
10th East Yorks	1000					Bde.
11th East Yorks	1000					Sewing machine, typewriter
12th East Yorks	1000		526			gramophone, records, tobacco
13th East Yorks	1000					song and dance music
East Riding Yeomanry	100					250 pairs of mittens, 50 comfort
140th (Hull) Heavy Battery	300					bags and 18 handkerchiefs.
1/3rd Northumberland Brigade, RAMC	1316					
St John VAD Hospital, Hull						
Sir Edward Ward, DGVO						
Total	6716	961	526	175	40	

Tobacco and cigarettes were sent to local units by the *Hull News* tobacco fund. With the demobilisation of the forces, the need for Paragon Rest Station was nearly over. It too would close down during the year. As a major port and railway terminal, Hull had large numbers of military personnel passing through in transit to their destination. This had put a strain on local resources even when facilities were open, and it was soon realised that the best way to deal with this transient population was a dedicated facility which was opened on 1 September 1914. From the commencement of its service, Paragon Rest Station was open twenty-four hours a day, providing shelter and refreshment to tens of thousands of men. Initially, everything was provided free of charge but as the cost of food rapidly increased, the sub-committee of the rest station was compelled to make the small charge of a penny, later rising to two-pence; expecting a decrease in use, the committee was pleased to find that the converse occurred.

After two years' work, the committee provided sleeping accommodation for stranded men. Thirty-four bunks were provided and fully equipped with bedding, through the kindness of the Ellerman-Wilson line, and for these a small charge of two-pence was made, while the North Eastern Railway Company provided the room, the heat and the light gratuitously. A buffet, at which sandwiches, pies and a variety of cake could be obtained, was also run. The station was exclusively staffed, night and day, for the first two years, by nursing members of the VADs of the St John Ambulance. After that time, they were assisted by voluntary female helpers.

Year	Number catered for
1914 & 1915	27,840
1916	108,741
1917	302,800
1918	322,950
1919	3,275
Total	765,606

Beds were found for 42,132 men during the war.

As there were fewer and fewer men needing a hospital bed, war-time-only facilities were closed. One of the first was Reckitt's Hospital, which ceased to operate in January. During the four years it was open, 2,910 patients passed through the forty-five bed ward at an average of thirty-five a week. At the same time the Lady Sykes' Hospital in France returned to Hull because the French no longer needed it. Brooklands Officers' Hospital was also closed down.

Most towns and cities set up VAD hospitals, indeed many such hospitals were set up in hotels, stately homes and any other large buildings that suited the task, and even schools were used. Hull was no exception. As well as a hospital, it was also necessary to set up a hospital supplies depot that dealt not only with the voluntary hospital but also with military hospitals and army hospitals abroad.

The following account, based upon the period 1918/19, is not atypical and gives a flavour of the work done.

'During the year the work of the Hospital increased steadily, and the total number of 4,933 were treated – in addition to the important work of the Out-patient Department – the average number of in-patients being 287, compared with 190 in 1917. The largest number in one day was 432. In the Out-patients' Department great developments have taken place, and surgical, massage, several kinds of electrical and Dowsing radiant heat treatment are now available. An electric switchboard was presented by the officers of the 5th (Reserve) Durham Light Infantry, and an electrical vibrator by the officers of the East Yorkshire Regimental Depot at Beverley, and a considerable amount of other apparatus has been purchased. Seven masseurs are now employed, and the total number of out-patient attendances for the year has been 4,390.

'The influenza epidemics of July and October put a severe strain upon the resources of the hospital, and upon the staff, many of whom were themselves ill; and it is greatly to their credit that the work was carried on efficiently in the face of such difficulties.

'During the autumn there were a number of repatriated prisoners (of war) who required hospital treatment before being sent to their home(s), and everything possible was done for them – the usual restrictions as to food, etc., being entirely relaxed.

'For their services to the hospital Mrs. Arthur Atkinson (Deputy Commandant), Sister Fanny Pease and Sister Lucy Brooks were awarded the Royal Red Cross, 2nd Class.

'As well as a hospital, St. John's Ambulance also ran a hospital supplies depot from September 1916 until the end of hostilities … During the two years and four months 138,210 articles were sent out – 24,206 to France, large numbers to Hull hospitals, St. John's Headquarters, and to Sir Edward Ward, Director-General of Voluntary Organisations. St. George's War Relief Committee in New York sent large consignments of garments, many of which were used to re-equip a bombed hospital in Boulogne. The depot was an expert manufacturer of a special dressing for the Carrel-Deakin treatment that they sent to Red Cross Hospital No. 9 in France.'

It closed on 20 December 1918, but, in response to an appeal by Sir Edward Ward to help the devastated areas of France, the depot collected and sent out just under 4,000 new garments of one type or another. In just over twenty-eight months, the depot had sent out 142,000 articles.

Money is nearly always the bottom line. While many families had suffered financially during the war, others had prospered. It was the same for companies. The turnover and net profit figures for Needler's show how well some firms benefited from the conflict.

Financial period	Turnover in £s	Net profit before tax in £s
April 1913-April 1914	95,4000	5,100
April 1914-April 1915	112,800	10,000
April 1915-December 1915	95,300	7,000 (9 months)
1916	171,100	17,500
1917	219,000	36,200
1918	446,700	101,300
1919	664,300	33,300

Two other major employers, Reckitt's and Smith & Nephew, increased their profits. In four years of war the staff of Smith & Nephew had increased from fifty to over 1,200. It had absorbed the whole of Neptune Street, bought a mill in Rochdale and formed a Manchester branch to make military equipment. During the war their total turnover was £2,500,000.

Conversely, Reckitt's complained about falling revenue in real terms. In 1913 their profit had been £580,730 paying a dividend of 27½ per cent on the ordinary shares. With the falling value of sterling, rising prices and wages, they estimated that the 1918 profit of £633,804 appeared to be more than 1913 but was actually worth less in real value. To improve profitability in 1918 they raised £2,178,000 with a £1 share issue. Throughout the war they maintained the dividend at 27½ per cent with 12 per cent on the 1918 issue.

However, they had benefited in a different way. German-owned companies became the property of the Custodian of Enemy Property, that is the Crown, and could be bought by British companies. Reckitt's bought two companies, Rawlins and Son which gave them control of ultramarine production in the country, and The Globe Metal Polish Co., a competitor with Brasso.

On the other hand, shipping had suffered considerably. By the end of the war only ninety-one Hull-owned ships were still afloat, and nine of these had been built during the war.

Companies now took stock of their manpower contribution to the armed forces and many published reports on casualties, awards and numbers enlisted. The report for Reckitt's gives an idea of the numbers involved for a large business. 'The immediate effects of the war on the company were the call-up of seventy employees, the billeting of troops on the Company's premises and the conversion of the 1907 Social Hall into a Military Hospital...By 1916 it was reported that 648 employees were in the forces and this figure had risen to 820 in 1917, when the number of fatal casualties was eighty.'

At the same time the number of employees rose from 4,761 in 1915 to 5,609 in 1917. By the Armistice, 1,100 employees were serving and 153 had lost their lives.

The war was over and the men returned, but there were still problems. A major issue for many was a job. The government offered its services through the Employment Exchange and asked firms to employ returned servicemen. Girls were asked to let ex-service men take their jobs. The government told employers: 'He risked his life for you. Are you going to give him a job? He will do it better. He will hold it more honourably, because he fought for it. This man who fought for you, and forged for you the Victory – and the Peace. The Employment Exchange brings the best man for the job into touch with the best job for the man…the Ministry of Labour is sparing nothing that shall make this the most efficient job-finding, man-finding machinery in the state.'

Those who had jobs to return to, like the writer's paternal grandfather, had no need for the Labour Exchange. He walked straight back into his highly skilled job on the Hull and Barnsley Railway. But the writer's maternal grandfather had a different experience. He was an eighteen-year-old conscript with no job to return to. Knowing just how employers would react to the return of such numbers of men, many of whom had no job saved for them, he elected to stay in the army and let the situation calm down before he returned to civilian life. Unfortunately for him, he arrived back in Hull shortly before the big crash.

In direct contrast to the exhortations of the government, Hull Council appointed a man who already held a job and who had not served with the colours. Mr Proctor had become the secretary of the City of Hull Great War Trust, at £8 a week, by the casting vote of the chairman of the panel. This naturally did not go down well with many in the city, who felt that there were many suitable ex-servicemen who were out-of-work who could have filled the position. A demonstration against the decision was organised for 10 May. At 2.30 pm a procession, headed by war-widows, marched from Corporation Field to hand in a petition containing 13,000 signatures to the Mayor. At a meeting 'charged with electricity', the Mayor told them he would do his duty and hand the petition to the committee. The procession reformed and marched through the town centre before breaking up.

There were other employment issues that the papers drew to everyone's notice. Some firms were not taking on men and were leaving women in employment and, worse still, there was a 'general apathy among Hull's public to the problem. One soldier had applied for reinstatement in his old job to be told: "We very much regret there is no vacancy at present".' Even City Hall was a problem. There up to twenty women were still employed while ex-servicemen, who were clerks, were drawing out-of-work pay. The same, ironically, was also happening in the Labour Exchanges.

This was not Hull Corporation's only issue. In early April a letter was presented to it, asking for a six-day week of forty-four hours rather than the current forty-eight, at the same wages as they were then being paid. It was not just a few workers. The letter was from the gas, electricity, water, tramways, highways, cleansing, parks, cemeteries and sewage farm departments. Their claim was successful.

Winning a VC gave the recipient a head start in getting a job. In April, Private Cunningham was recovering from wounds received in 1918. It was decided that it was a fitting opportunity to make an appeal for funds to the citizens of Hull, in order to give him a start in business. Accordingly, the Cunningham Fund was set up by the Sheriff and other city worthies.

Mention has previously been made of Hull's generosity, which was officially recognised by the offer of a tank to display. This was 'because of its high standard of patriotic achievement in National War Savings.' As it was such a great honour, the War Savings Committee accepted it unanimously.

Hull had received captured field guns and was set to receive a tank. It was decided that they should also have an aircraft, and the curator of the local war museum was instructed to apply for a small one. The fiasco over the wooden gun to protect Hull had not been forgotten, prompting one wit to write to the *Hull Times* about a further trophy for the museum. J.B. Anderson wrote: 'May I suggest that he [the curator] is also instructed to make application for the wooden gun set up for the defence of the city during the Zeppelin raids? It would be a standing memorial of the then authorities, under whose orders it was erected. All their names should be emblazoned on it in letters of gold. It would be a really interesting, unique, and historic addition – an example of "how NOT to do it".'

Easter was in late April and with the war now over for five months, the government relaxed rationing for the holiday. For the first time in years people in Hull could enjoy a hot cross bun. The Ministry of Food declared it 'had no objection to the manufacture of hot cross buns, nor to their sale when made less than twelve hours', as it did not consider that they came within the scope of the Bread Order, 1918.

Another Easter bonus came from the Food Controller. A licence was issued 'permitting the sale of chocolate and other sweetmeats for Easter eggs or toys or other like articles between 8 April and 23 April 1919 free from restrictions imposed by the Sugar Confectionery Order of

1917.' In addition Spanish onions were going down in price and enormous assignments of tea were arriving.

The food situation was, however, not improving as quickly as Hull wanted. While it was possible temporarily to buy luxuries like chocolate and hot cross buns, there were still shortages. As a result, there were still communal kitchens operating that Easter.

With PoWs repatriated, essential men released and general demobilisation proceeding as quickly as possible, it would not be long before the war service battalions were disbanded. For some there was little time to organise a homecoming. The arrival of the 7th Battalion was scheduled for 30 April but the city was not informed until the day before. With such short notice, the Mayor was unavailable so they were greeted at Paragon Station by Lord Nunburnholme. Of the cadre of forty-five men, twenty-three were from Hull. They were allowed home for the night, while the remainder were billeted in the city.

The next day, they went to the Regimental Barracks in Beverley. On arrival in Beverley they were met with enthusiastic cheering and marched off, to the tune of *The Yorkshire Lass*, to the barracks to hand over their colours. The 'streets were gay with flags and bunting and seemed as if the whole town was out to welcome them. A full parade of about 200 officers and men turned out to meet them with the depot band which arrived with minutes to spare.' They had been escorting the tank *Egbert* round West Hartlepool in recognition of the large amount they raised for the War Loan. The Mayor welcomed and thanked them on behalf of the people of Beverley. Headed by the band, the men formed into the military 'column of route' and marched by a circular route to the barracks. The colours were escorted, at the head of the column, by Lieutenant Stemple and Sergeants P.P. Taylor, MM and S. Slack. At the barracks they were given tea and the next day left for Ripon to be demobilised.

Although many wanted to forget, some still needed approbation for their contribution. The press were happy to oblige. One such family had their war effort explained in the 5 May edition of the *Hull Times*. 'Many local families have records of which they may be proud. No exception to this is the family of Mr and Mrs Braithwaite, 9 Princess Mary Avenue, Cleveland Street. This family of seven sons volunteered for service and six of them took part in the fighting. One of the sons is a corporal, three others are privates, two were naval gunners and the other a cadet. Unfortunately Mrs Braithwaite lost two of her sons, one being killed in 1914, when on board HMS *Bulwark*, which was blown up, and another son was killed in France. It cannot be said that this family has not done its share in the Great War.'

Ample time was given for preparations for the next units to arrive home. A week before their arrival, the Guildhall was being decked out with flags for the 10th and 11th Battalions East Yorks and 146 (Hull) Heavy Battery. Plans were carefully drawn up for the arrival of these special units. They would be met by Lord Nunburnholme and leading citizens at Paragon Station and treated to a civic reception at the Guildhall by the Mayor and Corporation. They would arrive from demobilising centres at Catterick and Sheffield, and then march to the Guildhall, accompanied by men already demobilised, along King Edward Street, Monument Bridge and Alfred Gelder Street. Music was to be provided by the police band.

On 26 May, to the sound of *Home, Sweet Home*, they marched through the cheering crowds who lined the route, after being welcomed by Lord Nunburnholme. The procession was headed by four officers and thirty-seven men from the 10th Battalion, followed by three officers and thirty-five men of the 11th and one officer and seventy-two men of the 146th Heavy Battery. There were two points of special interest in the parade: a German field cooker 'goulash cannon' – captured by the 10th and ex-Private Cotterell, of 3 Cobden Place, of the 11th Battalion, in a hand-propelled carriage.

From the Guildhall balcony the Mayor addressed the men. 'Now, boys. There is a banner on the Guildhall which says, "Well done Hull!" Today we give you a welcome as citizens of this great city.' After referring to labour difficulties he told them he hoped that employers would find employment for them. 'Men, you have fought a fight; you have gained a victory; you have won a peace.' As always there was a sting in the tail. 'We now require peace in our industry and a return to normal conditions and prosperity in trade.'

Before inviting the men to take light refreshments in the banqueting room, he had two further things to say. Firstly, 'I may sum up all I wished to say in two words. "Thank You." I give you a hearty welcome from the citizens of Hull, who are pleased to see you home.' The second must have struck at the hearts of most of those assembled. It was about a missing comrade. He told them he had received a letter and photo of

Private W. Loftus, A Company, 10th Battalion, who was reported wounded and missing. The writer had requested he exhibit the picture to the men 'with the hope that some of them might have good news.' Naturally, the Lord Mayor had his luncheon with the officers.

All that was left to come now were the peace celebrations. Although everybody knew the peace would be signed, there was no date set. Plans were discussed and made but final arrangements had to wait.

With the signing of the Versailles Treaty on 28 June the war was over. Two days later the Mayor sent a telegram to the king. 'Will your Majesty permit me on behalf of the citizens of Hull to offer their respectful congratulations on the termination of the war. Its conclusion affords the occasion of expressing the heartfelt thanks of the inhabitants to Your Majesty for your sympathy during the period of air raids made by our late enemy.'

The King replied, 'The congratulations you have sent me on behalf of the citizens of Hull on the conclusion of peace are of especial gratification to me, and in thanking you for this message I am fully mindful of the important and courageous part played by the inhabitants of your city during the long years that have ended in the triumph of our righteous cause. George R.I.'

Peace Day was fixed for 19 July and by Royal Command 6 July was Thanksgiving Day. Final preparations to celebrate began. Smith & Nephew would be able to contribute in an appropriate way and profit as well. At the end of the war the company had been left with large stocks of gauze cloth. To use this up, one third was left white, one third was dyed blue and one third red, and then sold as bunting.

The day started with a peal of the bells at Trinity Church and the town closed down for the celebrations. Although not lavish, the city was 'gay with flags'. In the working class areas displays were often extravagant and many had their own carnivals with fireworks, bonfires, music and children in fancy dress. In the parks there were band performances followed by fireworks. At East Park there was a boating costume carnival on the lake with prizes for the best costumes. Children received a Peace Souvenir book with a cover designed by Mr Trangmai of Hull Art Centre. A procession of about 3,000 men marched through the town from Walton Street Fair Ground, led by the naval contingent.

Rain in the evening dampened proceedings but it did not stop the fun. Many carried Chinese lanterns, the tramcars were illuminated and

Three of the German field guns given to Hull for display.

The march past of the 32nd Divisional Artillery Column at the Victory celebrations.

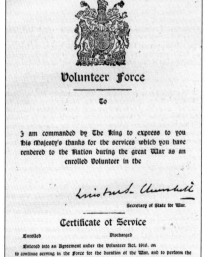

At the end of their service, instead of a medal, each volunteer received a certificate of service.

The Parrott Street Peace Party.

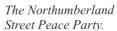

1st East Yorkshire Regiment soldiers in the Peace Parade.

The Northumberland Street Peace Party.

The Raglan Street Peace Party.

MENU

SOUP.
CONSOMMÉ SPRING.
CREAM OF TOMATO.
—
FISH.
BOILED TURBOT AND LOBSTER SAUCE.
—
ENTREE.
COLD GAME PIE.
—
JOINT.
ROAST LAMB AND MINT SAUCE.
—
VEGETABLES.
PEAS.   MARROW.   CAULIFLOWER.
ROAST AND MASHED POTATOES.
—
SWEETS.
VICTORY PUDDING.
BRAMBLE AND APPLE TART.
—
DESSERT.
—
COFFEE.

WENLOCK BARRACKS

EGYPT

HORNSEA.

FRANCE

SALISBURY PLAIN

HOME AGAIN

A Flag Day was one method used to raise funds for the Oppy Memorial.

Many veterans joined together to form Old Comrades Associations. The 10th East Yorkshire Regiment was quick to get together with its first annual meeting on 1 September 1919, five years to the day from when they were formed and only months after they had returned from France. This is the menu.

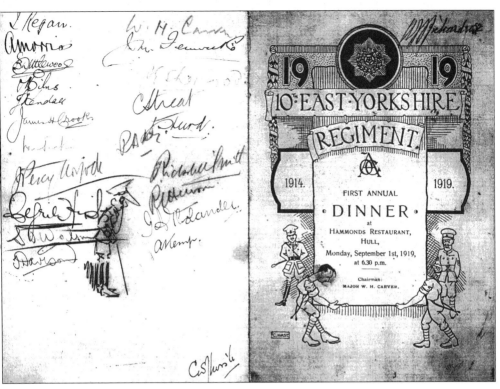

The front and back of the menu.

As the East Riding Royal Engineers were serving with a pre-war regular division when other Hull men were being demobilised they were sent to Germany as part of the occupation army.

The Hull Memorial on the edge of Oppy Wood.

Some Hull families had bad luck. Gunner Benjamin Bolton's father was killed during the war and he was killed in 1940 during the Blitzkreig.

fireworks were let off everywhere. Unfortunately, for many the firework finale 'was painfully reminiscent of Zeppelin nights.' In keeping with a celebration of peace, there was no rowdyism or vulgarity for the police to deal with.

The war was over and an anonymous, well-educated woman, a Manchester University graduate, had time to think about her experiences in Hull during the war and put them into perspective. Whilst many felt they had suffered, she was of a different opinion. 'Looking back, one realises how very little, in that war, the civilians had to put up with personally.' Reading her husband's war experiences confirmed her view. 'It made one feel how comparatively easy life on the Home Front had been.'

Appendices

TRAWLER LOSSES (BASED ON LOST TRAWLERS OF HULL)

Trawler name	Trawler No.	Date of loss	How lost
Imperialist	H.250	6.9.1914	Mined
St Lawrence	H.939	3.10.1914	Missing
Lorenzo (Admiralty)	H.865	17.12.1914	Wrecked
Tom-Tit (Admiralty)	H.35	26.12.1914	Wrecked
Celia	H 989	8.1.1915	Missing
Pamela	H.283	18.1.1915	Wrecked
Lord Londesborough	H.1021	17.2.1915	Wrecked
Kestrel	H.318	21.2.1915	Collision
Tern (Admiralty)	H.961	23.2.1915	Wrecked
Sapphire	H.675	1.3.1915	Mined
John Sherburn (Admiralty)	H.644	6.3.1915	Wrecked
Rhodesia (Admiralty)	H.443	19.4.1915	Wrecked
Columbia (Admiralty)	H.42	1.5.1915	Torpedoed
Mercury	H.518	2.5.1915	Gunfire
Bob White	H.290	3.5.1915	Gunfire
Coquet	H.831	3.5.1915	Bomb placed on board
Hector	H.896	3.5.1915	Submarine
Hero	H.886	3.5.1915	Bomb placed on board
Iolanthe	H.328	3.5.1918	Bomb placed on board
Northward Ho	H.455	3.5.1915	Bomb placed on board
Progress	H.475	3.5.1915	Bomb placed on board

Merrie Islington	H.183	6.5.1915	Bomb placed on board
Mauritius	H.547	17.5.1915	Missing
Duke of Wellington	H.388	18.5.1915	Torpedo boat action – crew taken prisoner
Euclid	H.370	18.5.1915	Torpedo boat action – crew taken prisoner
Titania	H.903	18.5.1915	Torpedo boat action – crew taken prisoner
Chrysolite	H.409	19.5.1915	Bomb placed on board
Angelo	H.890	21.5.1915	Mined
Sabrina	H.346	21.5.1915	Mined
Sebastian	H.888	22.5.1915	Missing
Southward Ho	H.456	27.5.1915	Missing
Dogberry	H.46	3.6.1915	Bomb placed on board
Bardolph	H.296	5.6.1915	Gunfire
Dromio	H.102	6.6.1915	Scuttled
Pentland	H.70	7.6.1915	Gunfire
Argyll	H.923	15.6.1915	Torpedoed
Quail	H.236	23.6.1915	Collision
Edison (Admiralty)	H.430	6.7.1915	Wrecked
Hermione	H.992	23.7.1915	Submarine
Sutton	H.363	23.7.1915	Gunfire
Cassio	H.889	24.7.1915	Gunfire
Emblem	H.301	25.7.1915	Gunfire
Honoria	H.325	25.7.1915	Gunfire
Langland	H.1013	16.8.1915	Wrecked
Lundy (Admiralty)	H.993	16.8.1915	Collision in Suvla Bay
Poonah (Admiralty)	H.737	18.8.1915	Collision in Suvla Bay
Commander Boyle	H.353	27.8.1915	Mined
Erin II (Admiralty)	H.757	19.10.1915	Mined
Lord Denman	H.118	22.10.1915	Collision
Scott (Admiralty)	H.968	22.10.1915	Mined
Bonar Law (Admiralty)	H.437	27.10.1915	Collision
Othello II (Admiralty)	H.956	31.10.1915	Mined

Princess Victoria (Admiralty)	H.766	7.11.1915	Collision
Edward B Cargill	H.412	15.11.1915	Mined
Malabar	H.754	27.12.1915	Missing
Speeton (Admiralty)	H.1011	31.12.1915	Mined
Onward Ho	H.935	5.1.1916	Missing
Cornelian	H.506	14.1.1916	Missing
Earl	H.436	21.1.1916	Missing
De La Pole (Admiralty)	H.377	4.2.1916	Wrecked
Flicker (Admiralty)	H.334	4.3.1916	Mined
Khartoum	H.472	26.3.1916	Mined
Hawk	H.389	19.4.1916	Collision
Osprey	H.64	18.5.1916	Bomb placed on board
Klondyke (Admiralty)	H.420	4.6.1916	Collision
Tugela (Admiralty)	H.521	26.6.1916	Mined
Staffa	H.814	10.7.1916	Bomb placed on board
Era (Admiralty)	H 461	11.7.1916	Submarine
Onward (Admiralty)	H.980	11.7.1916	Submarine
Bute	H.819	14.7.1916	Bomb placed on board
Irawadi	H.941	10.8.1916	Wrecked
Otterhound	H.92	24.9.1916	Submarine
Trinidad	H.336	25.9.1916	Submarine
Orsino (Admiralty)	H.864	28.9.1916	Submarine
Terrier	H.171	29.9.1916	Wrecked
Filey (Admiralty)	H.8	2.10.1916	Wrecked
Lord Roberts (Admiralty)	H.955	26.10.1916	Mined
Quair	H.237	3.11.16	Missing
Knot	H.784	5.11.1916	Wrecked
Anthony Hope (Admiralty)	H.1006	16.11.1916	Mined
Arran	H.820	18.12.1916	Gunfire
St Ives	H.11	21.12.1916	Mined
Teal (Admiralty)	H.90	2.1.1917	Wrecked
Shakespeare	H.994	7.2.1917	Submarine
Ireland	H.351	10.2.1917	Submarine
Hawk (Admiralty)	H.238	17.2.1917	Submarine

Halcyon	H.408	19.2.1917	Mined
Evadne (Admiralty)	H.945	27.2.1917	Mined
Redcap	H.962	1.3.1917	Gunfire
Christopher (Admiralty)	H.207	30.3.1917	Mined
Expedient	H.219	?.4.1917	Submarine
Industria	H.14	?.4.1917	Submarine
Gibraltar	H.1000	4.4.1917	Bomb placed on board
Caliban	H.313	12.4.1917	Gunfire
Equerry	H.36	12.4.1917	Gunfire
Martin II (Admiralty)	H.187	14.4.1917	Collision?
Erith	H.457	20.4.1917	Bomb placed on board
Lord Salisbury (Admiralty)	H.323	4.5.1917	Mined
Windward Ho	H.692	9.5.1917	Mined
Lucknow (Admiralty)	H.739	18.5.1917	Mined
Epworth (Admiralty)	H.386	22.5.1917	Collision
Towhee (Admiralty)	H.987	15.6.1917	Sank on escort duty
Fraser (Admiralty)	H.951	17.6.1917	Mined
Kelvin (Admiralty)	H.?	7.7.1917	Mined
Bovic (Admiralty)	H.51	5.8.1917	Collision
Jay (Admiralty)	H.278	11.8.1917	Submarine
Asia (Admiralty)	H.829	12.9.1917	Mined
Ruby (Admiralty)	H.494	17.10.1917	Submarine
Thomas Stratten (Admiralty)	H.116	20.10.1917	Mined
Commander Fullerton (Admiralty)	H.286	12.12.1917	Destroyer
Livingstone (Admiralty)	H.496	12.12.1917	Destroyer
Tokio (Admiralty)	H.954	12.12.1917	Destroyer
Duster (Admiralty)	H.267	17.12.1917	Wrecked
Miranda (Admiralty)	H.875	14.1.1918	Wrecked
Nerissa H (Admiralty)	H.879	28.2.1918	Wrecked
Agate (Admiralty)	H.2	14.3.1918	Mined
Vulture II (Admiralty)	H.470	16.1.1918	Eriboll Wreck
Swallow (Admiralty)	H.97	29.3.1918	Collision
Emiley (Admiralty)	H.384	28.4.1918	Mined
Eastward	H.1324	?.5.1918	Lost

Balfour (Admiralty)	H.432	13.5.1918	Collision
Egret	H.21	1.6.1918	Submarine
St Johns (Admiralty)	H.81	3.6.1918	Submarine
Eros	H.768	8.6.1918	Wrecked
Speedwell II (Admiralty)	H.481	15.7.1918	Wrecked
Sea Lark II (Admiralty)	H.407	30.9.1918	Collision
Neptunian (Admiralty)	H.626	27.10.1918	Collision

WILSON LINE LOSSES

Ship name	Date of loss	How lost
Castro	August 1914	Detained Hamburg, renamed Libau and scuttled 22.4.1916
Runo	5.9.1914	Mined
Truro	6.6.1915	Torpedoed
Guido	8.6.1915	Torpedoed
Grodno	12.8.1915	Mined
Serbino	16.8.1915	Torpedoed
Urbino	24.9.1915	Submarine
Salerno	14.10.1915	Mined
Colenso	30.11.1915	Torpedoed
Dido	26.2.1916	Mined
Teano	29.6.1916	Captured by submarine and scuttled
Calypso	10.7.1916	Torpedoed
Aaro	1.8.1916	Torpedoed
Ariosto	11.9.1916	Torpedoed
Thurso	27.9.16	Gunfire
Spero	2.11.1916	Torpedoed
Destro	25.3.1917	Torpedoed
Cannizaro	28.3.1917	Submarine
Salmo	7.4.1917	Torpedoed
Toro	12.4.1917	Torpedoed
Zara	13.4.1917	Torpedoed
Rinaldo	18.4.1917	Torpedoed
Cito	17.5.1917	Torpedo boat

Tycho	20.5.1917	Torpedoed
Oswego	29.5.1917	Torpedoed
Buffalo	18.6.1917	Torpedoed
Kelso	19.6.1917	Torpedoed
Cattaro	26.6.1917	Torpedoed
Torcello	15.7.1917	Torpedoed
Oslo	21.8.1917	Torpedoed
Erato	1.9.1917	Mined
Colorado	20.10.1917	Torpedoed
Carlo	13.11.1917	Torpedoed
Kyno	16.11.1917	Submarine
Cavallo	1.2.1918	Torpedoed
Jaffa	2.2.1918	Torpedoed
Polo	12.2.1918	Torpedoed
Romeo	3.3.1918	Torpedoed
Cicero	10.4.1918	Sunk to avoid capture
Montebello	21.6.1918	Torpedoed
Chicago	8.7.1918	Torpedoed
Idaho	19.8.1918	Torpedoed

AIR RAIDS (OVER FIFTY WARNINGS)

Date of raid	Where raid occurred	Casualties (numbers vary according to source, no official listing)
6 June 1915	Hull	25 dead, about 100 injured
5 March 1916	Hull	17 dead, about 60 injured
5 April 1916	Hull	Driven off
9 August 1916	Hull	10 dead, about 20 injured
3 September 1916	Hull	Driven off
21 August 1917	Hedon	No casualties
24 September 1917	Hull	3 casualties - injured
12 March 1918	Hull	1 died from shock

Bibliography

Anon. *Blundell, Spence & Co. Ltd. 1811-1951*. 1952.

Bilton, D. *The Home Front in the Great War*. Pen & Sword. 2004.

Bogie, J. *Mr Smith & his Nephew*. Smith & Nephew Medical Ltd. 1998.

Drake, R. *The Road to Lindi*. Reveille Press. 2013.

Eastern Morning News. Various editions 1914-1919.

Emsley, C. *Soldier, Sailor, Beggarman, Thief. Crime and the British Armed Services since 1914*. Oxford University Press. 2013.

Gill, Alec. *Lost Trawlers of Hull 1835-1987*. Hutton Press. 1989.

Gillett, E. & MacMahon, K. *A History of Hull*. Hull University Press. 1989.

Gurnham, R. *The Story of Hull.* Phillimore & Co. 2011

http://www.pocklingtonhistory.com

http://www.britishexecutions.co.uk

Kimberley, S. *Humberside in the First World War*. Local History Archive Unit. 1988.

Markham, J. *Keep the Home Fires Burning*. Highgate Publications (Beverley) Ltd. 1988.

Needler, R. *Needler of Hull*. Hutton Press. 1993.

Robinson, D. *The Zeppelin in Combat*. Foulis 3rd edition. 1971.

Russell, S. *More Heroes, Villains and Victims of Hull and the East Riding*. The Derby Books Publishing Company Limited. 2011.

Shakespeare, Lt. Col. J. CMG, CLE, DSO. *A Record of the 17th and 32nd (S.) Battalions Northumberland Fusiliers.* Northumberland Press Ltd. 1926.

Simmons, G. *East Riding Airfields*. Flight Recorder Publications Ltd. 2007.

Sumner, I. *'Despite It Not.' A Hull man spies on the Kaiser's Germany*. Highgate. 2002.

Taylor, J. *Ellermans. A Wealth of Shipping*. Wilton House Gentry. 1976.

The *Hull Daily Mail*. Various editions 1914-1919.

The *Hull Times.* Various editions 1914-1919.

White, J. *Zeppelin Nights: London in the First World War*. Bodley Head. 2014.

Wilkinson, A. (Ed.). *Thank God I'm Not A Boy*. Lampada Press. 1997.

Wright, J. D. *Young in Hull.* Malet Lambert High School. 1984.

Index